School Law

What Every Educator Should Know

A User-Friendly Guide

David Schimmel

University of Massachusetts

Louis Fischer

University of Massachusetts

Leslie R. Stellman

Johns Hopkins University

PEARSON

Boston • New York • San Francisco
Mexico City • Montreal • Toronto • London • Madrid • Munich • Paris
Hong Kong • Singapore • Tokyo • Cape Town • Sydney

Senior Series Editor: Arnis Burvikovs
Editorial Assistant: Erin Reilly
Marketing Manager: Danae April
Production Editor: Paula Carroll
Editorial Production Service: Omegatype Typography, Inc.
Composition and Prepress Buyer: Linda Cox
Manufacturing Buyer: Linda Morris
Cover Administrator: Joel Gendron
Electronic Composition: Omegatype Typography, Inc.

For related titles and support materials, visit our online catalog at www.ablongman.com.

Between the time website information is gathered and then published, it is not unusual for some sites to have closed. Also, the transcription of URLs can result in typographical errors. The publisher would appreciate notification where these errors occur so that they may be corrected in subsequent editions.

ISBN-10: 0-205-48405-0
ISBN-13: 978-0-205-48405-8

Library of Congress Cataloging-in-Publication Data

Schimmel, David.
     School law : what every educator should know : a user-friendly guide. / David Schimmel,
Louis Fischer, Leslie R. Stellman. — 1st ed.
          p.   cm.
     Includes bibliographical references and index.
     ISBN-13:   978–0–205–48405–8 (pbk.)
     ISBN-10:   0–205–48405–0 (pbk.)
   1.   Educational law and legislation—United States. 2.   Teachers—Legal status, laws,
etc.—United States.   I. Fischer, Louis   II. Stellman, Leslie.   III. Title.
     KF4119.8.E3S35 2008
     344.73'071—dc22

                                                                                    2007010008

Printed in the United States of America

10   9   8   7   6   5   4   3   2   1   12   11   10   09   08   07

about the authors

David Schimmel (J. D., Yale University) is Professor of Education in the Department of Educational Policy, Research, and Administration at the University of Massachusetts Amherst, and Visiting Professor at Harvard University's Graduate School of Education.

Louis Fischer (J. D. and Ph.D., Stanford University) is Professor Emeritus and former dean of the School of Education at the University of Massachusetts Amherst.

Leslie R. Stellman (J. D., Syracuse University) is chairman of an education law practice-group of a Maryland firm, as well as an Adjunct Professor of Education Law at Johns Hopkins University, Morgan State University Graduate School of Education, and the University of Baltimore School of Law.

brief contents

contents

3 *Responsibilities and Liabilities: Negligence, Libel and Slander, Child Abuse and Neglect*   *32*

Contents

5   *Student Freedom of Expression: Speech, Press, Association, and Appearance*   70

6 Due Process Rights of Teachers and Students   82

9   *A Teacher's Personal Life*   *121*

preface

A 2006 national survey of teachers found that the vast majority had taken no course in school law in their preservice or in-service programs, that they were seriously misinformed about key legal issues that confronted them in their classrooms, and that the major source of their legal information and misinformation was other teachers.[1] This survey of more than 1,300 teachers also revealed that over 65 percent wanted to learn more about teachers' academic freedom, student due process and discipline, liability regarding student injury, abuse and neglect, student freedom of expression, search and seizure, special education, employee rights, discrimination, and issues of religion and education. This book is designed to address these issues and clarify the confusions that too often surround these topics. It is about teachers and the law that affects them—law established by state and federal statutes, constitutions, and court decisions.

Our purpose in writing this book is not to encourage teachers to litigate. Going to court is expensive—emotionally and financially. Litigation tends to intensify conflict and polarize participants. Our goal is to help resolve educational conflicts without lawyers or courts. How? By helping teachers become *legally literate*—by providing them with information about the law that affects them, how the legal system works, and how that system can work for them in the public school. With this information, teachers can practice "preventive law." This does not mean that they will be their own lawyers, but rather that they will know their legal rights and responsibilities and will be able to educate other members of the school community about the law. Underlying this premise is our belief that unlawful school practices are generally not intentional but result from a misunderstanding about the law. Most school officials are anxious to avoid lawsuits; when teachers can show that a certain policy is illegal, administrators usually prefer to change the policy voluntarily rather than by a court order. We also believe that students' educational experiences improve when all members of the school community behave in a manner consistent with basic constitutional principles, such as due process of law.

Too many teachers view the law with anxiety and fear—as a trap to ensnare any educator who makes an innocent mistake, who disciplines a disruptive student, or who challenges an unreasonable parent. They see themselves as potential victims of a legal system that seems out of control. And they are excessively fearful about being sued. Much of this fear and anxiety is unfounded. It often is based on half-truths, misunderstanding, and misinformation about education law.

Teachers, for example, are unaware that in most states they are usually immune from personal liability when they have acted within the scope of their job duties, even if their actions (or inactions) result in injury to students or others. In addition, the federal No Child Left Behind Act protects teachers from being held liable for negligence when they discipline students or break up fights. Furthermore, many teachers do not know that recent court rulings have expanded their rights to be free from harassment and retaliation, to engage in "whistle-blowing" when they see law violations in the workplace or unequal treatment given to students based on gender, and to exercise their First Amendment freedoms of speech, religion, and association.

In short, the purpose of this book is to demystify the law for teachers by translating professional jargon and legalese into everyday English, and to empower educators to take the law constructively into their own hands. As a result, teachers will be able to use law as a source of guidance and protection, and have the knowledge needed to improve school and classroom rules, to assert their rights, and to bring violations of the law to the attention of administrators and colleagues. It is hoped that this book will be used in professional development programs and in-service workshops; will be a resource in professional libraries, teachers' rooms, and school offices; and will assist educators in making well-informed, legally sound decisions without fear of being sued.

Many teachers expect law to be fixed, clear, and unambiguous—like stop signs or the date school begins. Some is, but much of the law examined in these pages is neither simple nor unchanging. Many of the cases are as difficult to resolve for lawyers and judges as they are for educators. This is because cases involving school law often do not address simple conflicts of right against wrong, but rather complex issues encompassing the conflicting interests of teachers, parents, administrators, and students. Moreover, education law is constantly changing. New legislation is passed; regulations are amended; school boards revise their practices; and the Supreme Court denies or supports the constitutionality of particular policies. Because of this diversity and change, our discussion, while as current as we can make it, is intended to be illustrative, not exhaustive. We highlight major decisions and legislation of general interest to teachers rather than focus on legal details. Furthermore, we do not address all issues involving education law, only issues central to the daily lives of teachers. Citations to cases are in a form designed to be useful to teachers, rather than in the form used in legal treatises and law review articles.

This book is a condensed version of the seventh edition of our popular text, *Teachers and the Law,* (Allyn & Bacon, 2007). That text should be a useful resource for readers interested in a more extensive discussion of the cases and topics summarized in this guide.

How This Book Is Organized

Our first three chapters address the legal aspects of teaching and focus on questions related to teacher contracts, dismissals, tenure, collective bargaining, liability, child abuse, defamation, and copyright laws. Subsequent chapters focus on teachers' and students' rights and explore legal issues related to the scope and limits of personal freedom of expression, religion, and association; personal appearance, due process, and privacy. This also includes material on the right to be free from racial and sexual discrimination and rights related to school records; compulsory schooling, bilingual students, and students with disabilities; and the book concludes with a look at the No Child Left Behind Act and other current controversies.

The book follows a question-and-answer format. Most of the questions and answers are based on reported court cases. By introducing educators to the law through the use of real conflicts, we provide material to which classroom teachers may personally relate. We find that this type of format offers a more lively and effective way for teachers to relate to the law than does a focus on theoretical issues or legal abstractions. At the same time, each chapter goes beyond the outcome of specific cases and identifies the underlying principles that are likely to apply in similar cases in the future.

Books about law typically begin with a description of the legal system and court structure. Since such discussions are often hard to understand in the abstract, we introduce these concepts in the context of a case in which a teacher goes to court to protect his constitutional rights. The introductory chapter examines such questions as whether a teacher would bring suit in state or federal court, how he would identify the law relevant to his case, and how the case might be resolved.

Caution

Because the law is constantly changing and often varies from state to state, you should not rely on this book if you contemplate legal action. In such cases, you should first consult with your professional association or a knowledgeable lawyer.

But, since judicial resolution of an educational dispute is often an unhappy, expensive, difficult, and time-consuming process, bringing suit should be the last resort. We hope this book will help you resolve disputes through education, discussion, and negotiation rather than through litigation.

Request to Teachers

We want this book to work for you. By sending your comments, you can help us improve the next edition. What did you like and find useful? What should be added or eliminated? What was confusing or unclear?

Please send your reactions and suggestions to David Schimmel or Louis Fischer, 265 Hills South, University of Massachusetts, Amherst, MA 01003 (e-mail: schimmel@educ.umass.edu) or to Leslie Stellman, 25 Emerald Ridge Court, Baltimore, MD 21209 (e-mail: lrstellman@comcast.net).

Thanks from each of us.

Acknowledgments

We wish to acknowledge and thank Barbara Morgan, who provided invaluable research assistance in helping us find relevant cases, statutes, and articles.

We would like to thank Edward Biedermann and Tiffany Judkins for their insightful comments on the manuscript. In addition, we thank the following reviewers: Philip Bender, Indiana State University; Sandra Burvikovs, May Whitney Elementary School; Dr. Joseph Centamore, Rocky Point Middle School; Thomas Little, Kokomo School District; Katherine Lukaszewicz, Booker T. Washington Middle School; and Meghan Reilly, Andover Public Schools.

Note

1. David Schimmel, Matthew Militello, & H. Jake Eberwein, "Education Law Survey of Teachers," University of Massachusetts, Amherst, unpublished report (2006).

chapter 1

A Teacher's Perspective on the Legal System

The American legal system includes federal and state courts. The federal court system is based on Article III of the United States Constitution, which created a third branch of government to interpret the laws and declare whether laws enacted by Congress meet the requirements of the Constitution. They largely hear disputes between citizens of different states and arising under federal law or alleged breaches of the Constitution.

On the other hand, the state courts operate pursuant to the constitutions of each of the 50 states. They generally hear local disputes, including cases arising under state theories of negligence (called "torts") and contract law, and they interpret local and state laws. One of the important roles of state courts is to review determinations of administrative bodies such as local and state boards of education.

Each of the 50 states has at least one federal district court, although many larger states, such as New York, Texas, and California, have more than one federal courthouse, to ensure access to the federal courts for citizens throughout a state. Federal and state courts generally hear two types of cases: criminal and civil. This book will focus largely on *civil* litigation in both types of courts, for that is where the rights of teachers, students, and other members of the public that interact with schools are clarified, tested, and vindicated.

Pursuing a Civil Case in Court

How Does a Civil Lawsuit Work?

Lawsuits (whether filed in federal or state court) begin with the filing of a *complaint* alleging a violation of rights, an act of negligence, a breach of contract, or some other deprivation of rights recognized under the law. Suits can be filed by citizens or entities such as corporations, city governments or school boards. The person or entity filing a lawsuit is called the *plaintiff,* while the party defending the suit is called the *defendant.* Once the plaintiff files a complaint, the defendant is obligated either to file an *answer*—usually denying the wrongdoing or legal violation which the defendant is accused of committing—or a motion (called a "pleading") seeking dismissal of the complaint for failure to meet the minimum legal requirements of stating a valid basis for the lawsuit (otherwise known as stating a valid "cause of action").

For instance, a 5-year veteran teacher (we'll call him Ken) was an outspoken critic of the school board. Ken attended many public sessions of the school board, always signing up to speak during its "open forum," and always critical of board policies ranging from teacher salaries to what he called the "top-heavy, overpaid" administration. During his 5th year in the classroom, Ken took his complaints to a local radio talk show, whose host allowed Ken to speak for the entire hour-long program. Ken used the radio show to repeat his criticisms of the board, adding that he had evidence that certain board members were using their board-issued credit cards to buy expensive dinners and drinks at a local restaurant before each month's board meeting.

At the end of Ken's 5th year of teaching, the superintendent recommended that Ken be terminated due to incompetence, claiming that his lesson plans were disorganized, his instruction was poor, and his students' scores on high-stakes testing were below average.

Ken filed a complaint in federal court, alleging that the true reason he was being fired was his outspokenness against the school board and the exercise of his constitutional right of free speech.

Courts routinely dismiss lawsuits based on such motions where the plaintiff pleads insufficient facts to support the suit or relies on an unrecognized or discredited legal theory. (For instance, many lawsuits alleging "educational malpractice" have been routinely dismissed by the courts without trial, because virtually no state accepts the notion that such a "cause of action" exists under the law.) In Ken's case, there were sufficient facts pled in the complaint to withstand dismissal, at least initially. He claimed that: (1) he exercised his First Amendment right to speak out on matters of public concern; (2) that his public comments and radio appearance upset members of the school board as well as the superintendent; (3) that the superintendent thereupon set out to see that he would no longer work for the school system; and (4) that he lost his job because of the exercise of his constitutional and civil rights. In response, the board filed an answer denying that the decision not to renew Ken's contract was in retaliation for his outspokenness.

If the case is not dismissed in the initial pleading stage, the next stage of the lawsuit is called "discovery." This is a process in which each party learns as much about the other side's case as possible. Unlike the lawsuits of television and movies, there are generally no surprises by the time a case reaches trial and is heard by a jury.

Discovery consists of each party asking written questions (called "interrogatories") of the other side, demanding that the other side answer those questions in writing under oath and produce documents (including e-mails).[1] Each side can compel the other to admit to certain undisputed facts, which tends to shorten the time of trial because there are fewer disagreements about those facts. A common practice during discovery is for the parties to take the sworn testimony of witnesses identified by the other side. This process is known as conducting *depositions,* and involves bringing the witness into a lawyer's office in front of a court reporter and asking the witness questions, the answers to which may be used at trial. Even teachers who are not involved in a lawsuit have been ordered to sit for depositions, for instance in a divorce proceeding where parents are questioning a child's progress in school or a child's behavior.

In the case of Ken, his lawyer would ask, in a written request for documents, that the school board produce the contents of Ken's personnel file, his observations and evaluations, and any correspondence, including e-mails, that is in the possession of the board, the superintendent, or the school system, that in any way

● . . . .

4

addresses Ken's teaching performance and the reasons he was terminated. No doubt Ken's attorney will take the depositions of his principal, the superintendent, and members of the school board, while the board's attorney will want to depose Ken and other individuals he identifies as supportive of his case.

As with Ken's lawsuit, a great deal of litigation involving teachers is based on personnel decisions, like terminations, promotions, and harassment. Thus, personnel records, evaluation observations, and other documents reflecting a teacher's performance frequently become subject to discovery, while decision makers such as principals, human resources officials, and superintendents must respond to interrogatories, requests for production of documents, and depositions.

At the close of the discovery process, the defendant often asks that the judge dismiss the case based on the absence of any proof of a genuine dispute of material fact. This type of pleading is known as *summary judgment.* Most cases that get as far as the discovery stage still do not go to trial, for they are either settled or dismissed based on a motion for summary judgment, which means that at the close of discovery, the judge presiding over the case has concluded that the plaintiff has not demonstrated sufficient disputed facts to warrant the case going before a jury. In Ken's case, the board would support its motion for summary judgment with documentary evidence produced during the discovery phase of the case that provides legitimate reasons why Ken was terminated, such as poor evaluations and unsatisfactory classroom observations. If Ken cannot rebut this information, the court may grant summary judgment and dismiss his case before it ever gets to trial.

If the case is not settled or dismissed by the court, the parties finally go to trial before either a judge or jury, depending on the choice of either of the parties. Before the trial begins, attorneys for both sides submit proposed *instructions* to the judge, outlining their view of the law to be delivered to the members of the jury. Each side also proposes that the judge ask potential jurors specific questions intended to weed out biased individuals or jurors who might be too familiar with parties in the case or influenced by pretrial publicity. This process of vetting jurors is known as *voir dire,* or literally, "to see, to say." Jurors are selected from a jury pool by a combination of "for cause" and "preemptive" strikes by lawyers for each side. *For cause* means that a juror is disqualified for a stated reason approved by the judge, such as familiarity with one of the parties or witnesses or proven prejudgment of the outcome of the case. Each side is allowed a handful of *preemptive* strikes, which means that they can disqualify a potential juror without any reason. Once the alternate striking process has narrowed the number of jurors to 12 (or, in some jurisdictions, just 6), the trial begins.

Trials begin with each side's attorney presenting an opening statement of what they intend to prove. After witnesses testify and evidence is presented, the attorneys present closing arguments summarizing what they have shown during the trial, following which the judge instructs the jurors on the law they are to apply. It is at this point that jurors are informed about the so-called *burden of proof,* which is the measure of evidence one side or the other must put forth in order to prevail. In most civil suits, the plaintiff must prove its case by a *preponderance* of the evidence, which means that they must persuade the jury that they have demonstrated that there is a greater likelihood than not that what they set out to prove took place. (Contrast this to the much greater burden of proof that a prosecutor must show in order to successfully secure a criminal conviction, i.e., proof *beyond a reasonable doubt.*)

In Ken's lawsuit, he will have to convince a jury, by a preponderance of the evidence, that the reasons offered by the school board for terminating his employment were really a pretext for its true reason, which was to punish him for his public outspokenness against the board. If the jury finds that Ken has proven a causal connection between his public comments about the school board and the decision to terminate his employment, the jury could render a verdict that the board is liable for violating Ken's rights, and could award damages to Ken from the board and even from individual board members.

The jury selects a foreman and enters secret deliberations, which hopefully result in a unanimous verdict in favor either of the plaintiff or the defendant.[2] In most civil suits, the jurors must decide two things: first, whether the defendant is legally responsible, or *liable,* for violating the plaintiff's rights or for committing an act that caused the plaintiff harm. Then, if liability is found, they decide the amount of damages, if any, as the result of the defendant's actions. In employment discrimination cases, juries are empowered to award monetary damages, but only judges can award *equitable,* or *injunctive,* relief such as reinstatement to one's former job. In student rights cases, only a court can issue an order prohibiting the board of education from taking certain action such as continuing to conduct school prayers or censoring a student newspaper.

Litigants who lose at trial are entitled to have their cases heard by an intermediate court of appeals. However, to reach the Supreme Court of the United States or most states' supreme courts a petition for *certiorari* must be filed, which is a request that the high court hear the appeal. It is within the discretion of those courts, including the U.S. Supreme Court, to decide whether to hear a particular appeal. The Supreme Court may hear only about 80 cases from among the thousands of appeals filed each year.

How Can Teachers Find the Law?

Appellate courts issue both published and unpublished opinions, which may be located in courthouse law libraries found in most communities and universities. Teachers who have the citation to a specific case will be able to find it. The decisions of the highest appellate court, the U.S. Supreme Court, can be found in the official reporter the *United States Reports.* For example, the citation to *Brown v. Board of Education of Topeka, Kansas,* 347 U.S. 483 (1954), indicates that the case, decided in 1954, is reported in volume 347 of the *United States Reports* at page 483. Because Supreme Court cases are also reported in several commercial, unofficial publications, the same case may be followed by the notation "75 S. Ct. 753, 99 L.Ed. 1083." This means that the same case also appears in volume 75 of the *Supreme Court Reporter* on page 753 and in volume 99 of the *Lawyers' Edition* on page 1083. The most recent cases decided by the Supreme Court also appear online at www.supremecourtus.gov, under the hyperlink labeled "Opinions." Similarly, decisions of the federal appeals courts may be found in bound volumes published by West Publishing Company. For instance, a case called *Portland Public Schools v. Settlegood* is cited as "371 F.3d 503 (9th Cir. 2004)," which means that the case was decided in 2004 and is found on page 503 of volume 371 of *West's Federal Reporter, 3rd Series.* Decisions of the federal district courts are reported in the *Federal Supplement* and are similarly cited. For example, *Pyle v. South Hadley School Committee,* 824 F. Supp. 7 (D. Mass. 1993), a case involving the First Amendment right of students to wear controversial T-shirts to school, indicates that this case was decided by the federal district court for the District of Massachusetts in 1993, and is reported in volume 824 of the *Federal Supplement* on page 7.

Like decisions of the U.S. Supreme Court, state supreme court and state appellate court decisions are often published in more than one set of publications. One set is referred to as the "official reporter," and the other publications are referred to as "unofficial reporters." In New Jersey, for example, the official reporter is *New Jersey Reports* and the unofficial reporter is a regional volume known as the *Atlantic Reporter.* Thus, cases decided by the Supreme Court of New Jersey are reported in both publications and a full citation for a case would look like this: *Tibbs v. Board of Education of the Township of Franklin,* 59 N.J. 506, 284 A.2d 179 (1971). The "A.2d" indicates that this is the second series of the *Atlantic Reporter.* The original set of that *Reporter* is cited as "A."

Should a teacher seek out a certain state or federal law (statute), there are volumes containing the codes of all 50 states, while U.S. laws appear in the *United States Code Annotated* (U.S.C.A.). Publishers such as LexisNexis issue annual supplements to each state's laws, which are often contained in pocket parts in the back of the hardback editions of those publications. Lexis Nexis also publishes books containing state education laws and regulations for selected states, such as New York, Maryland, Virginia, Colorado, and Florida.

Teachers who lack a specific case name or citation can research the topic to find relevant cases through a variety of legal encyclopedias and digests, including *American Jurisprudence* (abbreviated as "Am. Jur."), *Corpus Juris Secundum* ("CJS"), or the West *Digest*. The *American Law Reports* ("ALR") provides lists of cases from around the country on a particular point of law. For instance, under "school teachers" one could find an annotation on "Sexual Conduct as Ground for Dismissal or Revocation of Teaching Certificate" (at 78 ALR3d 19). "Annotated statutes" include references to cases interpreting particular state or federal laws. Online the two leading legal research tools are Lexis and Westlaw, which require paid subscriptions. By entering key words into a search engine, those services will produce cases and statutes that contain those key words. Finally, West Publishing Company publishes a series titled the *Education Law Reporter* ("ELR") that contains every published federal and state court opinion addressing K–12 and higher education law, plus commentaries about school law cases and controversies.

Can Teachers Access Legal Websites?

Yes. To conduct legal research without charge, teachers may turn to Websites such as the Legal Information Institute established by Cornell Law School (www.law.cornell.edu) and www.findlaw.com. Many of the federal appeals courts as well as state supreme courts have Websites where they publish recently issued decisions. Many of the courts' Websites now allow visitors to access the actual oral appellate arguments made by the lawyers in each case.

Notes

1. Recent rules issued by the federal courts now require employers, such as boards of education, not to delete e-mails relating to the topics contained in the lawsuit, once the employer is on notice of the possibility of a lawsuit and the likelihood that e-mails will contain relevant evidence. Deleting e-mails is the twenty-first-century equivalent of shredding documents, and is now highly discouraged by lawyers and by the courts, which can issue severe sanctions to parties that ignore "do not delete" obligations.
2. In some state and federal courts, less than a unanimous verdict is sufficient, such as 4 of 6 or 9 of 12 jurors. Many federal courts empanel only six jurors in civil cases. A less than unanimous verdict usually requires agreement by both parties to the lawsuit when the jury is that size.

chapter 2

Teacher Contracts, Tenure, and Collective Bargaining

Local school boards have the legal authority to hire teachers, and most school boards have written contracts with their teachers. Local boards also have considerable discretion in deciding to whom they issue a contract, and for the first few years, who will be entitled to renewal of their contracts, which can lead to teachers acquiring tenured status. Once such status has been attained by years of continuous service, a teacher may only be terminated for a statutorily specified reason, such as misconduct in office, immorality, incompetence, or willful neglect of duty.

In a growing number of school districts, teachers and other workers are represented by labor unions that enter into collective bargaining agreements, or contracts that govern wages, hours, and other terms and conditions of employment such as planning periods, extra-duty pay scales for coaches, transfer and promotion procedures, or even class size and the length of the school calendar.[1] Because the provisions of school contracts as well as collective bargaining agreements vary tremendously, and because contract disputes can also require interpretation of various state laws, this chapter will briefly describe the basic legal principles surrounding the formation and termination of teaching contracts, the acquisition of tenure, and the role of labor negotiations and collectively bargained contracts in the lives of teachers.

Contracts of Employment

When Is a Contract Created?

"A contract is an agreement by two or more parties whereby obligations are created, modified, or extinguished. . . . A contract is formed by the consent of the parties through offer and acceptance, which can be made orally or in writing."[2] Certain requirements must be met before a contract is legally binding on both teachers and school officials. Like all contracts, a teachers' contract must have five elements: (1) a meeting of the minds of both parties; (2) valid consideration; (3) legal subject matter; (4) competent parties; and (5) definite terms.

In contract law, a *meeting of the minds* usually refers to mutual agreement to the terms of the contract. This agreement is usually reached through the process of offer and acceptance. *Consideration* refers to the promises bargained for or exchanged between the parties. To have valid consideration to support a contract, each party must give up something of value; that is, the parties must promise to do something they are not legally obligated to do or to refrain from doing something they are legally permitted to do. In the case of a teaching contract, consideration consists of the exchange of promises between the teacher and the school; the teacher promises to perform certain teaching services, and school officials promise to pay the teacher a certain salary. For instance, teachers who give up a summer vacation in order to teach summer school have offered consideration by relying on the promise of the school board to hire them for the summer. Even without a written contract, this reliance may be sufficient to support a binding and enforceable contract between the teachers and the school system.

Legal subject matter means that the contract cannot require the parties to act in a manner that violates public policy. For instance, a contract would not be valid if it broke the law, such as a contact that forces a teacher to give up the right to a state's minimum wage. *Competent parties* means that the people contracting must be of legal age (usually 18), and must have the mental capacity to understand the terms of the contract. *Definite terms* means that the contract must be clear enough so that each party knows what the contract requires. Like other employment contracts, a teaching contract that does not state either salary or teaching duties is too indefinite to be legally enforced. Thus, an Indiana court held that a contract to pay a teacher "good wages" was not valid.[3] In addition, state law may provide that the school board must ratify a contract before it is legally binding.

Express and Implied Contracts

Does a Contract Have to Be in Writing?

No. Unless state law requires that a teacher's employment contract be in writing, an oral contract that has all the necessary legal requirements is legally binding.

What Is a "Unilateral" Contract, and Can It Be Legally Binding?

A unilateral contract arises from a promise made by one party in exchange for the other party's act or performance.[4] For instance, when a school district offered to employ a bus driver, the offer did not solicit a return promise from the driver (and none was given). Because an offer for a unilateral contract is accepted by performance, the school district was not contractually bound until the driver actually commenced driving. Until that point the school district was free to revoke the offer any time prior to acceptance.[5]

Can an Employee Handbook Serve as a Basis for Contractual Obligations?

Possibly, if the handbook does not contain a disclaimer explicitly denying that it serves as a contract of employment.[6] In such cases, handbooks have been found not to be legally binding contracts. When an employee is working without a formal employment contract, the terms of an employee handbook may be contractually binding. Although some courts reject this idea, judges in most states recognize the contract potential of employee handbooks and manuals. An employee handbook creates enforceable contractual rights if the traditional elements of contract formation (offer, acceptance, and consideration) are satisfied.[7] Courts have held that not every policy pronouncement made in a personnel handbook or other publication will rise to the level of an enforceable contract. For a handbook provision to have contractual force, it must be specific and clear, the employees must be aware of it and believe it to be an offered term of employment, and they must continue to work after notification of the term, thus giving consideration.[8]

How Long Does a Contract Last?

Normally a contract states how long it is to be in effect. Nontenured teachers generally hold their positions under annual contracts, whereas tenured teachers may be employed under "continuing contracts." Most states allow school boards to enter into multiyear employment contracts with teachers, as well as multiyear collective bargaining agreements with unions representing teachers, bus drivers, custodians, and other groups of school employees.

Can a Nontenured Teacher Be Renewed Automatically from Year to Year?

Yes, if the local school board fails to provide timely notice to the nontenured teacher of its intent not to renew the teacher's contract. Most state laws provide that by a certain date (usually in April or May), the school district must inform a 1st- or 2nd-year teacher, in writing, of an intent not to renew his or her contract; failure to do so has been found to be grounds for automatic renewal of the contract for another year.[9]

Can Teachers Work without a Contract?

Yes, but by doing so teachers may have more difficulty proving what their compensation should be. Thus, an Illinois court held that tenured teachers who failed to sign new contracts would not be entitled to wages and benefits offered to teachers who signed their contracts.[10] If teachers work without a contract, they may be entitled only to pay based on a theory of *quantum meruit,* or payment for the estimated value of services rendered.

Breach of Contract

How Can a Contract Be Broken by School Officials?

A contract is binding on both parties, and either party who fails to meet contractual obligations has *breached* (broken) the contract. School officials who attempt to change the terms of a contract after it is in effect, for instance by removing extra duties (and attendant pay) from a teaching assignment, have breached the contract. The remedy ordered by the court in that instance was restoration of the teacher's extra-duty salary.[11]

How Can a Teacher Break a Contract?

The same principles that apply to school officials also apply to teachers. A teacher who has signed an employment contract and then refuses to accept the teaching position or abandons the position in midyear has breached the contract and may be subject to monetary penalties or even license forfeiture, depending on state law.[12]

What Are the Legal Consequences of Breaking a Contract?

When one party breaches a contract, the other party to the contract is entitled to a legal remedy, called *damages,* that will compensate for the injury the breach has caused. Thus, when a school board breaks an employment contract, the injured teacher is entitled to damages in the form of salary owed under the contract less any interim earnings from another position. Damages may also include expenses incurred in relocating or finding another teaching position. Although generally damages do not include legal fees, attorneys' fees and costs of a lawsuit may be awarded in cases based on discrimination or First Amendment claims.

When the School Board Breaches a Contract, Must a Teacher Look for Another Teaching Position to Collect Damages?

Usually yes. This is called the "duty to mitigate damages," and a teacher who does not look for another job may not be entitled to money owed due to the breach. However, a teacher is not obligated to take a job in another locality or accept an inferior position in order to avoid loss of damages due to a breach.

Can a Court Order a School Board to Rehire a Teacher?

Yes, where an award of money will not adequately compensate the teacher, or where the teacher unjustly lost a tenured position. Discrimination victims or teachers who were found to have been wrongly fired for exercising constitutionally protected rights are entitled to reinstatement.

Are There Other Ways the Contract Can End?

Yes. If a contact's terms can no longer be performed, like a teaching assignment in New Orleans immediately following Hurricane Katrina, this is known as *impos-*

sibility of performance, which excuses either or both parties from carrying out its terms. If a contract is the product of both parties' misunderstanding of the facts when entered into, it may not be enforceable. Some states recognize an "implied obligation of good faith and fair dealing" in the performance of an employment contract. Where a community college president admitted to working in another job while on the college's payroll, the college was deemed entitled to discontinue paying her salary for breach of that duty.[13]

What Is Tenure?

Tenure is a legal means of protecting the economic and job security of teachers. Tenure confers the right to express our views, even when they are unpopular, without undue fear of administrative reprisal. Tenure ensures that teachers cannot be terminated except on proof of just cause. Teachers who are granted tenure can be dismissed only for a cause set out by law, such as incompetence, immorality, and willful misconduct, although this does not guarantee a teacher a specific position or building assignment in a school district, or even indefinite employment. Before tenured teachers can be dismissed, school boards must show cause why they are not fit to teach. Tenured teachers are also entitled to notice of charges against them and a hearing in which the board has the burden of proving that there is legal cause for dismissal. Most tenure rights are contained in state laws, but in addition, teachers' rights derive from the due process clause of the U.S. Constitution. Regardless of whether a teacher has tenure, the U.S. Supreme Court has held that teachers who have constitutionally protected interests in property or liberty are entitled to notice and a hearing prior to termination.

How Do Teachers Acquire Tenure?

There are generally two ways that teachers acquire tenure: by law or by "custom," as in the Supreme Court's landmark case of *Perry v. Sindermann,*[14] in which a community college professor with nearly 10 years of experience was afforded the right to a hearing before being removed even though he was not covered by a tenure law. When a teacher such as Professor Sindermann can prove an expectancy of continued employment, she or he has a property interest in job tenure that is protected by the due process clause of the Fourteenth Amendment.

In most situations, state law establishes a teacher's right to tenure. Most state laws outline the requirements for tenure. Usually, such laws require teachers to first undergo 2 or more years of probationary status, during which period they are employed under a series of renewable 1-year contracts. In some states, such as Maryland, a 3rd year of probation may only be permitted if a teacher demonstrates some promise of continued growth and is assigned a mentor by the school district. In some states tenure is automatic after a certain amount of time, but in others the school board must approve tenured status. Tenure may be conditioned upon meeting certain requirements, such as passing the National Teachers Examination (NTE),[15] obtaining a state teaching certificate, or becoming "highly qualified" under the federal No Child Left Behind Act.

Can a Teacher Be Awarded Tenure If School Officials Fail to Follow Required Legal Procedures?

It depends on the state. Failure to give proper notice to a teacher of her nonrenewal resulted in an award of tenure by a Kentucky court[16] and a Colorado court ruled that untimely notice of nonrenewal entitled a teacher to tenured status.[17]

How Else Can a Teacher Acquire Tenure?

In addition to a right to tenure under state law, a teacher may also have a right to tenure under an employment contract that describes in specific terms the teacher's right to continued employment and sets out detailed procedures that must be followed before the teacher can be dismissed.

Is There a Condition under Which Tenure Can Be Denied Even When the Teacher Has Served the Requisite Number of Years?

Yes. For instance, if teachers continuously failed to successfully complete all the sections of the National Teacher Examination, or otherwise fail to become certificated or eligible to receive "highly qualified" status under the No Child Left Behind Act, they can lose their tenured status. This applies to teachers who fail to continue taking courses necessary to maintain their credentials.

Can Other School Employees Acquire Tenure?

Most state laws provide that only full-time certificated or professional employees acquire tenure. The definition of exactly which employees are required to have certification can vary from state to state. For instance, some states do not acknowledge tenure beyond that of a classroom teacher, which means that administrators such as principals and department chairpersons do not acquire tenure of title or tenure of position. Administrators can therefore be reassigned to classroom teaching positions without the necessity of demonstrating "cause," except in those states where tenure is granted to administrators in their administrative positions or even to specific building assignments. Most extra-duty assignments like coaching positions are subject to 1-year contracts, which means that teachers may be removed from those assignments without proof of "just cause."

Can a State Do Away with Tenure?

Yes. When state law creates a right to tenure, it can usually take this right away. Many teachers' contracts include a provision stating that a teacher's tenure status is subject to change or termination according to any changes in the state law. Even if a teacher's contract does not include such a provision, courts have ruled that state legislatures have the power to modify their teacher tenure laws, thus possibly depriving a teacher of tenure. In Wisconsin, for instance, the court upheld the legislature's power to repeal the Teachers' Tenure Act.[18] Similarly, a federal appeals court ruled that the Chicago School Reform Act's repeal of principals' tenure was permissible, explaining that tenure was a right created by statute and that a statute is presumed not to create contractual rights.[19] Once tenure is acquired, however, some courts have refused to allow a state law to remove that status from a teacher even after tenure has been repealed.[20]

Teachers may be furloughed, laid off, and even terminated for economic reasons despite enjoying tenured status. This could include the elimination of a particular program due to declining enrollment or because of a failure to fully fund the school budget.[21]

Rights of Tenure

What Rights Does a Tenured Teacher Have?

A teacher who achieves tenured status has the right to continued employment subject only to dismissal "for cause." Similarly, a nontenured teacher who is terminated during the contract year, rather than not renewed at its completion, may invoke the same rights as a tenured teacher to be afforded reasons for the dismissal and a complete evidentiary hearing. The teacher does not have the right to be employed in a particular position, however. School boards and superintendents of schools retain the authority to transfer and reassign even tenured teachers, provided that they are assigned to comparable positions, the decision to reassign them is consistent with the best interests of the schools, and is neither arbitrary nor discriminatory.[22]

Courts have ruled that tenured teachers can be reassigned as part of desegregation plans. In cases of school districts under such plans, the courts have denied the right of school boards to use tenure laws as an excuse to resist transferring teachers to achieve racial balance.[23] Nor does tenure prevent a teacher's salary from being reduced for budgetary or other reasons, provided that such reductions are applied uniformly to all teachers and salary schedules remain fixed until the end of a school year absent a financial emergency.[24]

Dismissal Procedures

When Can Tenure Be Broken?

School officials can dismiss a tenured teacher only for "cause." Teacher tenure laws generally list specific offenses that constitute legal cause for dismissal, and school officials can dismiss a teacher only for one of these reasons. For example, Maryland law permits the termination of teachers for one of five enumerated reasons: incompetency, misconduct in office, willful neglect of duty, insubordination, and immorality.[25] Other states have additional or alternative bases, including "conduct unbecoming a teacher" and "inefficiency."[26]

Usually courts have held that tenured teachers can be dismissed only for "something of a substantial nature directly affecting the rights and interests of the public . . . one touching . . . the performance of her duties, showings he is not a fit or proper person to hold the office."[27] In examining the nature of the offense attributed to a tenured teacher to determine if there is sufficient cause to dismiss, there must be a proximate relationship, called a "nexus," between the offense and the teacher's fitness for duty. Many negotiated contracts governing teachers' employment contain clauses protecting teachers from being dismissed due to personal lifestyle choices or other activities that are unrelated to their teaching performance.

What Procedures Have to Be Followed before a Tenured Teacher Can Be Dismissed?

Most states provide for specific procedures before tenured teachers can be dismissed. Typically these statutes require that teachers be given notice of the charges against them and an opportunity for a hearing at which they can respond to those charges. In order to ensure a fair hearing, the following steps ought to be taken, consistent with constitutional and statutory requirements found in most states' tenure laws:

1. There should be a statement of charges and the basic information on which those charges are based.
2. If requested, a hearing ought to be held before the school board, a hearing panel, or a hearing officer designated by the school board.
3. Timely written notice of the date, time, and place of the hearing should be provided.
4. A hearing in public or, if requested by the teacher, in private should be held.
5. The teacher should have an opportunity to be represented by counsel and to present a defense to the charges.
6. There should be an opportunity to call witnesses on the teacher's own behalf.
7. In many (but not all) states, the teacher has an opportunity to subpoena any person who has made allegations that are used against the teacher as a basis for the termination recommendation.
8. There should be an opportunity to cross-examine witnesses presented against the teacher.
9. Witness testimony should be made under oath or affirmation.
10. A record should be made (preferably by a certified court reporter) of the proceedings so that it may be reviewed by a higher authority.
11. A written decision that contains specific findings of fact, conclusions of law, and grounds on which the decision is based should be rendered.
12. A written statement of the teacher's right to appeal should be provided.[28]

All testimony is given under oath, and the local or state board of education must pay a court reporter to make a written record of the hearing so that the record may be reviewed by the courts. When either the state law or local board policy governing dismissal of tenured teachers prescribes a specific procedure, it must be followed exactly. For instance, failure to follow board policy requiring that at-risk teachers be afforded mentoring and assistance, including a professional improvement plan, before being discharged, has resulted in the reinstatement of a tenured teacher.[29]

Courts have generally held that it is not a denial of constitutional due process to suspend a tenured teacher without pay while disciplinary proceedings are pending, provided that the hearing is not unduly delayed. Due process viola-tions have been found where the hearing lacked impartiality,[30] or where the same school official acted as both prosecutor and hearing officer.[31]

What Notice Must Be Provided to a Tenured Teacher Prior to Dismissal?

The courts have required that clear statements of the charges be given to tenured teachers so that they can answer those charges. Merely informing a teacher that she was guilty of "insubordination," for instance, was deemed insufficient be-cause it did not inform the teacher of facts on which she could reasonably mount a defense: "It gives no date of her actions, nor does it indicate in any way the specific nature of her acts."[32] Similarly, because the board had notified a teacher only that her services "had been unsatisfactory and incompetent," an Alabama court ruled that a teacher could not be dismissed since the board failed to give the teacher any specific information describing her "incompetency."[33] More spe-cific charges must be leveled against a tenured teacher, in writing, for them to be deemed specific enough to warrant dismissal, such as:

- poor relationship with other teachers;
- lack of cooperation with the principal and the guidance staff;
- poor attitude and a disruptive influence; and
- not in harmony with the educational philosophy of the school.[34]

Even these reasons have been found lacking in other states. Courts may also be critical of school systems that fail to fully inform teachers of their deficien-cies before termination. In a Missouri case, for instance, a tenured teacher who was terminated for incompetency based on detailed notes taken by her principal, which were never previously shown to the teacher, was reinstated by the court, because the "school administration knew what the instances of alleged incom-petence were, but [the teacher] did not. Had she been informed in advance of the specific and particular instances of alleged incompetence, she could have been prepared to contradict them or to explain them."[35]

Do Teachers without Tenure Have a Right to Notice and a Hearing Prior to Nonrenewal of Their Contracts?

Not usually. In the words of one court, "a school board has unfettered discretion when deciding whether to renew the contract of a probationary teacher."[36] Some states give nontenured teachers minimal procedural rights, but generally require that teachers prove that their nonrenewal was arbitrary, discriminatory, or illegal. "Paper reviews," that is, examinations only of teachers' school performance records, tend to be conducted by boards of education in such appeals rather than full-fledged hearings with witnesses and the introduction of evidence. In Illinois, nontenured 2nd-year teachers are entitled to notice of the reasons for nonrenewal, while in Connecticut nontenured teachers must make a special written request in order to receive a statement of the reasons why the board decided not to renew their contract. Many states require that a minimum number of observations be conducted before the contracts of nontenured teachers are not renewed.

What Constitutional Protections Apply in Cases of Teacher Dismissal?

Regardless of the procedures required under the state law, the U.S. Supreme Court ruled that teachers are entitled to notice and a hearing if their termination deprives them of *property* or *liberty* interests under the due process clause of the Fourteenth Amendment to the U.S. Constitution. In *Board of Regents v. Roth,*[37] the Court defined these terms: "To have a property interest in a benefit, a person clearly must have more than an abstract need or desire for it. He must have more than a unilateral expectation of it. He must, instead, have a legitimate claim of entitlement to it." The Court went on to explain that property interests are not created by the Constitution. "Rather, they are created and their dimensions are defined by existing rules or understandings that stem from an independent source such as state law—rules or understandings that secure certain benefits and that support claims of entitlement to those benefits."[38] In *Roth,* the teacher involved had been hired under a series of one-year contracts, so the Court concluded that he had no such interest in reemployment as to establish a property interest that would entitle him to procedural rights under the Fourteenth Amendment.

In *Roth,* the Supreme Court also held that teachers are entitled to due process protection if their dismissal deprives them of a "liberty" interest under the Fourteenth Amendment. In interpreting this term, the Court included "the right of the individual to contract, to engage in any of the common occupations of life."[39] The Court explained that a violation of this "right" could occur by taking action that would foreclose a teacher's opportunities for employment, stating that a liberty interest would be involved whenever the school board, in declining to rehire a teacher, made a charge that might seriously damage the teacher's reputation, such as charges of dishonesty or immorality. In the Court's words: "[W]here a person's good name, reputation, honor, or integrity is at stake because of what a government is doing to him, notice and opportunity to be heard are essential."[40] When a school district publicizes stigmatizing disciplinary charges, the employee's "liberty" interest is implicated and a name-clearing hearing may be required if requested by the teacher. However, courts have ruled that due process does not require a hearing before an employing school district publishes stigmatizing reasons for a teacher's discharge.[41]

Grounds for Dismissal

What Constitutes Cause for Dismissal?

State laws, local school board policies, and collective bargaining agreements contain specific reasons why tenured teachers can be dismissed. Some reasons identified by state law for dismissal include insubordination, incompetence, and misconduct.

When Can a Teacher Be Fired for Insubordination?

Teachers cannot be dismissed for insubordination unless they deliberately defy school authorities or violate reasonable school rules. For an order to be reasonable, school officials must have the legal authority to issue it. Some courts have found insubordination in a single incident, such as a teacher who called in "sick" to attend an interview for another job, whereas others have concluded that insubordination can only occur when there is a constant or persistent pattern of conduct. In one New Mexico case, the court upheld dismissal of a teacher who threatened to call the police if the principal did not leave her classroom, while ripping lesson plans out of the principal's hands.[42]

For a rule to be reasonable, it must be clear enough for teachers to understand. Merely refusing to "cooperate" with a principal was deemed insufficient grounds to fire a teacher for insubordination.[43] But a teacher who flatly refused to transfer to another school was deemed insubordinate and subject to dismissal. Similarly, a federal appeals court upheld the termination of a tenured teacher who refused to cooperate with her principal by meeting with him to discuss teaching deficiencies and who occasionally left the building without informing anyone of her whereabouts.[44]

When Can a Teacher Be Fired for Incompetency?

An incompetent teacher is one who cannot perform the duties required by the teaching contract. But a teacher who delivers a poor lesson on only one or two occasions cannot be dismissed for incompetency. In order to fire a teacher, school officials generally have to present a number of examples of the teacher's inability to meet contractual responsibilities. School districts in most states, however, are required to work with and attempt to remediate the performance of a poorly performing teacher before terminating the teacher. Whether this requirement is the result of state law or regulation, or whether it is included in a collective bargaining agreement or even the individual teacher's contract, courts tend to strictly enforce this obligation.[45]

The clearest example of an incompetent teacher is one who lacks knowledge about the subject he or she is supposed to teach. A Louisiana third-grade teacher was dismissed for incompetency when her supervisor "noted many mistakes in her grammar and in her punctuation."[46] Teachers may also be unable to teach. Given the duty of employers under the Americans with Disabilities Act to offer disabled employees "reasonable accommodations" in order to enable them to perform the "essential functions of their job,"[47] a school district should first explore every reasonable and available accommodation to ensure that a disabled teacher may, with or without assistance, be able to continue teaching. Thus, a court held that an Indiana school district could not accuse an individual of poor performance when the district was aware of the employee's mental disability but made no effort to find out what he needed to enable him to work.[48]

When a school psychologist prepared poor reports and conducted inadequate testing, she was properly dismissed for incompetence, whereas a Maryland teacher was lawfully terminated for both misconduct and incompetence when he ignored established procedures for disciplining students despite prior warnings, refused to meet with his principal, and delivered repetitive, poorly planned lessons.[49]

When Can a Teacher Be Fired for Immoral Conduct?

In the past, teachers were expected to teach morality through their actions, and when teachers violated community norms, they lost their jobs. Teachers have been fired for lying, cheating, talking about sex, using "obscene" language, public drinking, drug use, homosexual conduct, and having a child out of wedlock. The definition of "immoral" conduct varies in different communities. Today teachers can still be fired for immoral conduct, but in most cases such conduct must be linked to a teacher's effectiveness. Sexual misconduct with a student is assuredly an act of immorality that would warrant termination under any state's tenure law.[50] Circulating racist jokes was held to be an act of immorality, since such behavior served as a poor role model.[51] (For more on this topic, see Chapter 9.)

A companion to sexual contact but just as appropriate a basis for a finding of immoral conduct is a teacher's sexual harassment of students and even other teachers. Such conduct also violates Title VII of the Civil Rights Act and possibly Title IX of the Education Amendments, subjecting the school district to monetary penalties and other consequences.

Are There Other Reasons for Teacher Dismissal?

Yes. Many state laws provide that teachers can be dismissed for "good and just cause," "conduct unbecoming a teacher," "willful misconduct," or "neglect of duty." These catchall phrases give school boards wide discretion, effectively allowing them to dismiss teachers for reasons not specifically listed under state law. As one court explained, "good cause includes any ground which is put forward by the [board] in good faith and which is not arbitrary, irrational, unreasonable, or irrelevant to the [board's] task of building up and maintaining an efficient school system."[52]

The courts have imposed limits on school officials' power to dismiss teachers for "good and just cause," insisting that the action must bear a reasonable relationship to fitness or capacity to discharge the duties of the teaching position, especially when it involves off-duty conduct. In rejecting the dismissal, on immorality grounds, of a teacher who engaged in an act of homosexual conduct with another consenting adult, the California Supreme Court insisted that the following facts be considered when establishing a rational nexus between a teacher's off-duty conduct and his job:

- the likelihood that the conduct may have adversely affected students or other teachers;
- the anticipated degree of such adversity;
- the proximity or remoteness in time of the conduct;
- the extenuating or aggravating circumstances, if any, surrounding the conduct;
- the likelihood of the recurrence of the questioned conduct; and
- the extent to which disciplinary action may have a chilling effect on the constitutional rights of the teacher involved or other teachers.[53]

Collective Bargaining

What Is Collective Bargaining?

Collective bargaining brings together individual employees to advance their collective interests in better wages, hours, and terms and conditions of employment.

Teachers have a constitutional right to join a union. Whether they have a right to engage in collective bargaining, however, depends on state law. Today over 40 states have passed laws guaranteeing that public employees have a right to engage in collective bargaining. These laws generally provide that public school teachers have the right to organize and join employee labor organizations, and that they can select representatives of their choosing to bargain with their employer about wages and working conditions.

State laws vary considerably. Some states merely require boards of education to "meet and confer" with teacher organizations, whereas others allow for bargaining over many conditions of employment, including class size, the school calendar, and the length of the workday. In most states, disputes arising under the union contract may be resolved by binding arbitration.

How Are Collective Bargaining Laws Enforced?

To enforce collective bargaining for public employees, many states have established labor relations boards. These boards certify unions as the lawful representatives of teachers and ensure that both sides comply with the duty to bargain. There is no federal law that specifically regulates collective bargaining for teachers, except for teachers employed by U.S. Department of Defense schools, who are covered by federal labor relations laws.

Is There a Constitutional Right to Organize?

Yes. In addition to state laws giving teachers the right to join unions, the courts have ruled that the U.S. Constitution's protections of free speech and freedom of association give teachers the right to organize.

Is There a Constitutional Right to Bargain?

No. Most states have statutes that provide for collective bargaining for teachers, but in the absence of such laws, teachers do not have a constitutional right to bargain collectively.

Who Decides Who Will Represent Teachers in the Collective Bargaining Process?

State laws that provide for collective bargaining for teachers generally also establish a procedure to decide who will represent them in negotiations with the school board. Typically, the laws state that the board must bargain with the organization that a majority of teachers in the district designates as the exclusive representative, a process that is usually accomplished in a secret election conducted by state labor relations officials.

Do All Teachers Have to Join the Employee Organization Selected as the Exclusive Representative?

No. Public employees cannot be forced to join a union as a condition of their employment (the so-called *union shop* or *closed shop*). Some state laws recognize this right, stating that employees have a right to join or to refuse to join or participate in the activities of employee organizations.

The U.S. Supreme Court has ruled that the First Amendment gives teachers who are not union members the right to make public comments about matters that are the subject of collective bargaining negotiations without fear of reprisal either from the board or their union.[54]

Can Teachers Who Are Not Union Members Be Required to Pay Fees to a Union?

Yes. Over half of the states have passed laws that permit "agency-shop" or "fair share" arrangements under which employees who are not members of a union can be assessed fees to a union as a condition of their employment. The Supreme Court has ruled that such an arrangement is constitutional, noting that they properly defray the union's cost of collective bargaining and contract enforcement.[55]

Can Teachers Be Required to Support Union Political Activities?

No. The Supreme Court has ruled that it is a violation of the First Amendment to require a public employee to pay dues to support a union's political activities. However, the Court noted that there would be "difficult problems in drawing lines between collective bargaining activities, for which contributions may be compelled, and ideological activities unrelated to collective bargaining, for which such compulsion is prohibited."[56]

What Are a Union's Legal Responsibilities as the Exclusive Collective Bargaining Representative for Teachers?

The employee organization that acts as the exclusive bargaining agent also has a legal duty to represent all teachers in that bargaining unit, regardless of membership. This *duty of fair representation* prohibits the union from discriminating against any of its members in the negotiation and administration of collective bargaining agreements. In addition, the union must represent the interests of all members of the bargaining unit—even those who are not union members—in the negotiation process. This duty requires the union to be honest and fair but does not deprive it of discretion in deciding how to negotiate with the school board or how to handle teachers' grievances. Unless the union is acting in "bad faith" or discriminatorily, it is not a violation of this duty for a union to refuse to pursue a grievance.

The union also has the obligation to bargain with the school board in *good faith*. This means that the union must meet at reasonable times and places to negotiate with the school board and to make a sincere effort to reach an agreement on the topics under discussion. Good faith does *not* require either party to reach an agreement or to make any concessions on a particular issue, but it does mean that neither side can merely go through the motions of meeting with the other. Both sides must consider and respond to each other's proposals. Examples of bad-faith bargaining include refusing to bargain with the designated representative or refusing to participate in mediation required by the terms of the contract or state law.

Can a Union Have Exclusive Access to School Mail Facilities?

Yes. The Supreme Court has held that there was no violation of teachers' First Amendment rights when a school board agreed to limit access to faculty mailboxes to the union designated as the exclusive bargaining representative.[57] The Court reasoned that the school mailboxes did not constitute a public forum and therefore could be limited to official school business, including business of the designated union representative of the teachers. Rival union groups could still communicate with the teachers via other methods, such as bulletin boards and mailings.

What Legal Responsibilities Does a School Board Have in the Bargaining Process?

A school board has the same legal duty to bargain in good faith as a union. For the school board, this duty includes the obligation not to make unilateral changes in wages, hours, or other terms and conditions of employment without first bargaining with the union and either reaching agreement on the change or an impasse. For instance, when faced with declining revenue a school system cannot simply ignore provisions of the contract guaranteeing no layoffs or furloughs without first bargaining with the union before implementing either cost-saving option.

Can a School Board Bypass the Union and Make Salary Agreements with Individual Teachers?

No. The school board must bargain exclusively with the teachers' designated representative over wages, hours, and other terms of employment. It is deemed an *unfair labor practice* (or violation of the bargaining law by either side) for a school district to enter into individual arrangements with certain teachers and to agree to pay them different wages than the other teachers who are covered by the union contract.[58] Even if teachers asked for these changes, the school district cannot bypass the union.

Contract Negotiations

What Happens During Collective Bargaining?

The bargaining process can begin when a contract is about to expire and either the school district or the union wishes to negotiate a different agreement. Usually the process commences with an exchange of proposals between the parties, followed by discussions over each proposal. Each side generally designates a chief negotiator who acts as a spokesperson, but in more collaborative forms of bargaining, such as "interest-based" bargaining conducted in many school systems, all parties at the negotiating table are encouraged to participate fully in the discussion.

What Kinds of Subjects Are Discussed at the Bargaining Table?

Examples of topics that are routinely included in the bargaining process are:

- Compensation: cost-of-living adjustment, salary schedule, pay for specific duties (department chair, coach), minimum teacher salaries, expenses, travel reimbursement, tuition reimbursement, mentor teacher selection process
- Benefits: health and welfare premiums, retiree benefits
- Hours: length of workday, work year, student year, calendar (holidays, vacations), minimum days, preparation periods, lunch
- Leaves: bereavement, pregnancy, child rearing, religious, sick leave, disability, sabbatical, personal need/necessity, jury duty, military, catastrophic illness
- Retirement: early retirement, benefits

- Job assignment: assignment, promotion, transfer, reassignment
- Class size and caseloads: pupils per teacher, students per counselor, number of teaching periods, instructional aides
- Safety conditions
- Evaluation: procedures and remediation
- Grievance: procedures, appeal process, mediation, arbitration
- Discipline: procedures and criteria
- Layoff and reemployment

Are There Limitations on the Scope of Collective Bargaining?

Yes. First, the parties cannot enter into contractual negotiations that are in violation of a state constitutional provision or state and federal laws. For instance, in states such as Maryland which ban teacher strikes, the subject of such strikes is deemed illegal, and is thus off limits for discussion or agreement. If an agreement is reached over the "illegal" subject, the resulting provision of the contract is unenforceable. Some topics, however, are considered "permissive" under certain states' bargaining laws, which means that they need only be discussed if both sides willingly agree to do so. Neither side can force the other to discuss, much less reach agreement on, a "permissive" subject. In Maryland, teacher transfers is an example of a "permissive" subject.

What Happens If a Union and a School Board Cannot Agree on a Contract?

State procedures vary for when unions and school boards reach an *impasse* in bargaining. States with laws that merely require school boards to "meet and confer" with unions do not have any procedures for resolving a deadlock in negotiations, while states with mandatory bargaining laws often provide detailed impasse procedures that may culminate in a binding or nonbinding recommendation by a neutral fact finder. This is known as *interest arbitration* (as opposed to *grievance arbitration,* in which a neutral third party issues a binding interpretation of the contract). The most common process for resolving these disputes is *mediation,* in which the parties meet with a neutral third person or persons who attempt to resolve their differences through discussion and by proposing compromise provisions. The mediator merely functions as a facilitator and has no legal power to force either party to accept his or her suggestions or to make a concession.

Strikes

Do Teachers Have the Right to Strike?

The right of teachers to strike varies from state to state. Most states prohibit teachers (and most other public employees) from engaging in strikes. Illinois, Pennsylvania, and other states allow for such strikes, but usually only after certain steps have first been taken, including mediation.

What Penalties Can Be Imposed on Teachers Who Engage in an Illegal Strike?

Some state laws stipulate penalties that may be imposed on teachers and their union, ranging from individual fines for strikers (often at the rate of a day's pay for each day a teacher is on strike, thus discouraging teachers from striking) to fines and even jail sentences for union leaders. Other penalties include denying striking unions the right to continue as the exclusive representative of the teachers for a certain penalty period (such as 1 year) or preventing them from collecting dues.

In addition to the sanctions described in state laws, courts have ruled that school boards have certain options available in strike situations. School officials can ask the courts to issue an injunction to prohibit the strike. The union, its officers, and members can be held in contempt and fined or jailed if they remain on strike in violation of a court order to return to work.[59]

Finally, courts have ruled that school boards can impose economic sanctions on teachers who go on strike. A New York court upheld the constitutionality of a state law that allowed the board to make payroll deductions in the amount of twice the daily rate of pay for each day a teacher was on strike.[60] Similarly, a Florida court ruled that a school board could lawfully fine teachers $100 as a condition of reemployment following an unlawful strike.[61] In 1991, an Indiana court ruled that an elementary school student could not sue for damages allegedly sustained when her teachers participated in an illegal strike. The court held that only the school board could bring an action against the union for conducting the strike.[62]

Guidelines

- Teachers' rights are created either by contract or by state law, including the right not to be terminated except for certain enumerated causes. Most states have passed tenure laws that give teachers the right to continued employment once they have satisfactorily completed 2 or 3 years of probationary service. State legislatures have the power to repeal or change these laws.

- While enjoying protection from arbitrary termination, most teachers and administrators do not enjoy tenure of title or position. This means that they may be reassigned with little or no due process and for virtually any reason the school district chooses.

- Teachers initially sign single-year contracts that may be renewed at the discretion of the superintendent or board of education. During a teacher's probationary period this 1-year contract may be renewed or not, with or without cause. Due process protections, including the right to an evidentiary hearing, generally only apply to teachers who are tenured.

- State laws, often in conjunction with collective bargaining agreements, describe procedures to be followed before a tenured teacher can be dismissed, as well as specific grounds that must be demonstrated in order to justify terminating a tenured teacher. Courts have insisted that tenured teachers be given adequate warning about their behavior and its likely consequences. If boards of education adopt policies or procedures for assisting poorly performing teachers, such as offering teachers additional training, modeling by master teachers, and assistance in lesson planning and instructional delivery, those procedures must generally be followed before terminating a tenured teacher for incompetence.

- Many teachers are members of a union, which enjoys the right to bargain over wages, hours, and other terms and conditions of employment with representatives of the school district. While most states prohibit strikes by teachers, many have impasse procedures intended to facilitate agreements between teachers' unions and boards of education.

Notes

1. Some states, such as Maryland, prohibit negotiations or contract provisions governing certain subjects such as the school calendar and class size, considering such subjects to be within the authority of the board of education, but other states allow it.
2. *Loup v. Louisiana Sch. for the Deaf,* 729 So.2d 689 (Ct. App. La. 1999).
3. *Fairplay Sch. Township v. O'Neal,* 26 N. E. 686 (Ind. 1891).
4. *Greene v. Oliver Realy,* 526 A.2d 1192 (P.A. Super. 1987).
5. *Kuhnhoffer v. Naperville Cmty. Sch. Dist.,* 758 F. Supp. 468 (N.D. Ill. 1991).
6. *Conkwright v. Westinghouse Electric,* 739 F. Supp. 1066 (D. Md. 1990).

7. *Duldulao v. Saint Mary of Nazareth Hosp.*, 505 N.E.2d 314 (Ill. 1987).

8. *Univ. of Baltimore v. Iz*, 716 A.2d 1107 (1998).

9. *Noxubee Cnty. Sch. Bd. v. Cannon*, 485 So.2d 302 (Miss. 1986).

10. *Davis v. Bd. of Educ. of Aurora*, 312 N. E.2d 335 (Ill. Ct. App. 1974).

11. *Lowder, et al. v. Minidoka County*, 979 P.2d 1192 (Idaho 1999).

12. *Bd. of Educ. of Talbot County v. Heister*, 896 A.2d 342 (2006), which provided for "liquidated damages" in the form of forfeiture of salary not yet paid but still owed to teachers who abandoned their position before the start of the next school year.

13. *Harmon v. Adirondack Comm. Coll.*, 784 N. Y. S. 2d 663 (3d Dept. 2004).

14. 408 U.S. 93 (1972).

15. *Cooper v. Norris*, 2000 WL 173209 (Tenn. Ct. App. 2001).

16. *Harrodsburg Bd. of Educ. v. Powell*, 792 S. W.3d 376 (Ky. Ct. App. 1990).

17. *Day v. Prowers County Sch. Dist. RE-1*, 725 P.2d 14 (Colo. Ct. App. 1986).

18. *State ex rel. McKenna v. Dist. No. 8*, 10 N. W.2d 155 (Wis. 1943).

19. *Pittman v. Chicago Bd. of Educ.*, 64 F.3d 1098 (7th Cir. 1995).

20. *Indiana ex rel. Anderson v. Brand*, 305 U.S. 95 (1938). To avoid this result, some legislatures may "grandfather" existing tenured teachers under statutes intended to abolish the status, as in *Costello v. Governing Bd. of Educ. of Lee Co. Special Educ. Ass'n.*, 623 N.E.2d 996 (Ill. App. 1993).

21. *Baltimore Teachers Union v. Mayor of Baltimore*, 6 F.3d 1012 (4th Cir. 1993); *Gross v. Bd. of Educ. of Elmsford Union Free Sch. Dist.*, 78 N. Y. 2d 13, 574 N. E.2d 438, 571 N. Y. S.2d 200 (1991).

22. *Hurl v. Bd. of Educ. of Howard Cnty.*, 667 A.2d 970 (Md. 1995).

23. *United States v. Bd. of Educ. of City of Bessemer*, 396 F.2d 44 (5th Cir. 1968).

24. *Compton Cmty. Coll. Fed. of Teachers v. Compton Cmty. Coll. Dist.*, 211 Cal. Rptr. 231 (Cal. Ct. App. 2d Dist. 1985).

25. *Annotated Code of Maryland*, Education Article § 6–202(a) (LexisNexis 2005).

26. *New York Education Law* § 3020a (McKinney's 2005).

27. *State ex rel. Richardson v. Board of Regents*, 261 P.2d 515 (Nev. 1953).

28. E. M. Bridges & B. Groves, *Managing the Incompetent Teacher* (ERIC Clearinghouse on Educational Management, 1984).

29. *Bd. of Educ. v. Ballard*, 67 Md. App. 235, 507 A.2d 192 (1986).

30. *Keith v. Cnty. Sch. Dist. of Wilton*, 262 N. W.2d 249 (Iowa 1978), where the Board chose to call no witnesses, relying instead on its "collective recollection" of the facts.

31. *Osborne v. Bullitt Cnty. Bd. of Educ.*, 415 S. W.2d 607 (Ky. Ct. App. 1967).

32. *Id.* at 567.

33. *Cnty. Bd. of Educ. v. Oliver*, 116 So.2d 566 (Ala. 1977).

34. *Sparks v. Bd. of Educ.* 549 S. W.2d 323 (Ky. Ct. App. 1977).

35. *Jefferson Consolidated Sch. Dist. v. Carden*, 772 S. W.2d 753 (Mo. Ct. App. 1989).

36. *Johnson v. Indep. Sch. Dist.*, 479 N. W.2d 392 (Minn. Ct. App. 1991).

37. 408 U.S. 564 (1972).

38. *Id.* at 577.

39. *Id.* at 572.

40. *Id.* at 573 (quoting *Wisconsin v. Constantineau,* 400 U.S. 433 (1971).

41. *Rankin v. Indep. Sch. Dist.,* 876 F.2d 838 (10th Cir. 1989).

42. *Kleinberg v. Bd. of Educ. of Albuquerque,* 751 P.2d 722 (1988).

43. *Osborne v. Bullitt Cnty. Bd. of Educ.,* 415 S. W.2d 607 (Ky. Ct. App. 1967).

44. *Berg v. Bruce,* 112 F.3d 322 (8th Cir. 1997).

45. *Bd. of Sch. Commissioners of Baltimore v. James,* 625 A.2d 361 (1993).

46. *Singleton v. Iberville Parish Sch. Bd.,* 136 So.2d 809 (La. Ct. App. 1961).

47. 42 U.S. C. § 12112 (LexisNexis 2005).

48. *Bultemeyer v. Fort Wayne Cmty. Sch.,* 100 F.3d 1281 (7th Cir. 1996).

49. *Nichols v. Caroline County Bd. of Educ.,* 2004 WL 350337 (D. Md.), *aff'd* 114 Fed. Appx. 576, 2004 WL 2699962 (4th Cir. 2004).

50. *Strain v. Rapid City Sch. Bd.,* 447 N.W.2d 332 (S.D. 1989).

51. *Reitmery v. Unemployment Comp. Bd. of Review,* 602 A.2d 505 (Pa. Cmwlth. Ct. 1992).

52. *Rinaldo v. School Comm.,* 1 N. E.2d 37 (Mass. 1936).

53. *Morrison v. State Bd. of Educ.,* 82 Cal. Rptr. 175, 461 P.2d 375 (1969).

54. *Madison Jt. Sch. Dist. v. Wisconsin Emp. Relations Comm.,* 429 U.S. 207 (1977).

55. *Chicago Teachers Union v. Hudson,* 475 U.S. 292 (1986).

56. *Abood v. Detroit Bd. of Educ.,* 431 U.S. 209 (1977).

57. *Perry Educ. Ass'n. v. Perry Local Educ. Ass'n.,* 460 U.S. 37 (1983).

58. *Bd. of Educ. v. Ill. Educ. Labor Rel. Bd.,* 620 N. E.2d 418 (Ill. App. Ct. 1993).

59. *In re Block,* 236 A.2d 1589 (N.J. 1967).

60. *Lawson v. Bd. of Educ.,* 307 N.Y.S.2d 333 (N.Y. Sup. Ct. 1970).

61. *Nat. Educ. Ass'n. v. Lee Cnty. Bd. of Public Instruction,* 299 F. Supp. 834 (M.D. Fla. 1969).

62. *Coons v. Kaiser,* 567 N.E.2d 851 (Ind. Ct. App. 1991).

chapter 3

Responsibilities and Liabilities

Negligence, Libel and Slander, Child Abuse and Neglect

*L*iability is a concept of civil "fault" in which a person or entity (like a board of education), acting by itself or through others, causes harm to another. While the criminal courts deal with questions of "guilt" or "innocence," courts that hear civil cases are focused on determining who is legally responsible for an accident or injury. This is known as determining liability. A *tort* is an act that injures someone and for which the injured person may sue the wrongdoer for damages. There are two types of torts: intentional ones, such as libel and slander, and negligence, which is unintentional.

Determining Liability for Torts

School board members and employees, including teachers, may be liable for negligence, but in most states they are protected by statutory *immunity* where their negligence arose during the course of their employment. One area in which teachers are generally not protected by immunity is when they engage in acts of child abuse, including sexual abuse, or in many states, when they fail to report such abuse once it is discovered.

When Can Teachers Be Held Liable for Negligence?

The courts and state legislatures have generally imposed on teachers a mandatory duty to supervise students under their control. Individual teachers may be held liable for damages to an injured student if the student can prove four things: (1) the teacher had a duty to be careful not to injure the student; (2) the teacher failed to use due care; (3) the teacher's carelessness caused the injury; and (4) the student sustained provable damages. Usually in cases of student injury, it is easy to prove that a teacher had a duty to be careful toward his or her students, and that the injuries resulted in monetary damages. Sometimes there is a question about what precisely caused the injury. In most cases, the critical question is whether the teacher violated his or her duty of care and therefore was negligent.

A teacher who, for instance, takes his students on a field trip and then leaves one of them "in charge" while visiting with a friend, is negligent and would probably be held liable if one of his charges gets hurt. Or a coach who fails to properly instruct her students in the safe use of gym equipment will be deemed *liable* for negligence, perhaps even *gross negligence,* a finding with even greater legal and liability consequences for the teacher. Teachers are not expected to anticipate every situation in which a child may get hurt, such as a fight that suddenly breaks out among students, and most injuries are due to accident and not negligence. However, *reasonable care* is expected, which means that teachers are held to a standard of what a reasonable teacher with ordinary prudence would have done under the circumstances. Thus teachers are negligent if they fail to act reasonably prudent under the circumstances. When circumstances may be dangerous (e.g., in a chemistry laboratory or on an overnight trip) closer supervision and clearer warnings are usually prudent, especially for younger students.

The concept of *duty of care* was applied in a Maryland case to hold two guidance counselors liable for failing to attempt to prevent a student's suicide.[1] In that case, the father of a 13-year-old student sued the counselors when his daughter consummated a murder-suicide pact with another 13-year-old. He alleged that his daughter had told several friends she intended to kill herself and that the friends had told the counselors, who talked with the daughter but failed to alert the parents. In imposing a duty of care on the guidance counselors, the court held that there was an affirmative duty to inform the parents, who might have been able to intervene.

A student whose parents alert the school that their child is allergic to certain foods or environmental factors in the school may be able to assert a claim for negligence if teachers and other school personnel allow that student to be exposed, thereby suffering injuries. Under federal disability rights laws, discussed later in this book, schools may have to reasonably accommodate a student's food or other allergies, ensuring that the child is not likely to be exposed.

Are Teachers Required to Supervise Their Students at All Times?

Not always. According to a Minnesota court, there is generally "no requirement of constant supervision of all movements of the pupils at all times."[2] However, a teacher would have a duty to provide constant supervision under dangerous conditions, especially among young children.

But when a 12-year-old student was fatally injured playing a dangerous skateboard game at an unlocked elementary school playground long after school had let out for the day, the court said that schools do *not* have a duty to supervise the grounds at all times. On the contrary, the duty of supervision is limited to school-related or -encouraged activities that take place during school hours. "To require round-the-clock supervision or prison-tight security for school premises," wrote the court, "would impose too great a financial burden on the schools."[3]

Can a Teacher's Duty of Supervision Extend Beyond School Hours?

Yes. Teachers are not ordinarily liable for students' acts after school, but they can be held liable if they assign or initiate dangerous activities, such as encouraging a science project that, when done unsupervised at home, proves to be dangerous.

Can Teachers Be Held Liable If a Student Injures Another Student or a Teacher?

Yes. If a teacher knows or should know that a student is likely to harm another student or a teacher, the teacher has an obligation to try to prevent the injury. For instance, where a teacher was overheard saying, "there you go again" when a student lifted a smaller child and threw her into a fence, causing serious injuries, the teacher and school board can be held liable, since such comments reflected foreknowledge of the larger child's propensity to engage in precisely the same type of violence.[4] Neither the school board nor the wrestling coach were liable, however, when a student member of the wrestling team, after losing a match, threw a chair that injured a spectator. The court held that there was no pattern of violence on the part of the student that would have put the faculty or school board on notice of the student's propensity to act inappropriately.[5]

Can Teachers Be Held Liable If a Classroom Aide Injures a Student?

Not if the teacher exercises ordinary care in supervising the aide. When a teacher's aide in a special education class severely beat a child while the child and aide were in the bathroom, the court found that there was no evidence that the teacher knew that the aide was beating the student or that she could have foreseen such an action, so the teacher was deemed not liable.[6]

If Teachers Are Careless, Are They Automatically Liable for Damages?

No. To recover damages, injured students must prove more than that the teacher was careless; they must also show that the teacher's failure to use due care was the cause of the injury. For example, in cases where children were injured while playing with their fellow students while waiting for the bus, courts have generally deemed the teachers not to be liable because there was no way to prove that careful supervision would have prevented the injury. "As is often the case," concluded one such court, "accidents . . . involving school children at play happen so quickly that unless there was direct supervision of every child (which we recognize as being impossible), the accident can be said to be almost impossible to prevent."[7]

When a student jumping for a basketball bumped heads with another student, causing him injury, his father's lawsuit against the school board for failing to adequately supervise the game was dismissed on the grounds that the presence of a teacher would not have necessarily prevented the boys from bumping their heads during the basketball game. Thus, the court concluded, even if the absence of supervision constituted negligence, it was not the proximate cause of the accident.[8]

Are There Special Liability Standards for Substitute Teachers and Student Teachers?

No. Substitute and student teachers are held to the same duties of care as full-time teachers and would be liable for foreseeable injuries that are caused by their negligent acts. A substitute was found liable for failing to adequately supervise a shop class when one student sexually assaulted another student behind a portable chalkboard in the classroom.[9] However, a substitute or student teacher would not be liable for damages resulting from a student's unforeseeable behavior, as in the case of a sixth-grade student who was injured because a classmate pulled his chair out from under him as he went to sit down. In that case, there was only one aide supervising two classrooms, there had been no reason to expect any behavioral problems with such an arrangement, and the injury was the result of an unexpected prank that could not have been anticipated or prevented.

Defenses against Liability

Injured students who sue teachers and administrators for damages may encounter the defenses of contributory or comparative negligence, assumption of the risk, or governmental immunity.

What Is Contributory Negligence?

If a student's own negligence contributed to the injury, the law in a few states would consider the student guilty of *contributory negligence,* which would bar him or her from any recovery of damages, even if his or her negligence only played a small role in causing the injury. Where, for instance, a student injured herself in a shop class by placing her hands in a machine contrary to instructions about safe practices, she was barred from recovering damages under this theory. Evidence indicated that the teacher had demonstrated the safe use of power tools, had designed a safety booklet for students to read, had given a safety exam, and had watched the student operate the machine safely. Though the teacher apparently failed to adequately supervise the class, the student was denied recovery due to her own negligence.[10]

Does a Student's Age Affect His or Her Right to Recover for Negligence?

Yes. The younger the student, the more difficult it is to prove contributory negligence. In most states, courts hold that very young children, typically those under

7 years of age, are incapable of contributory negligence. This means that even if the carelessness of such students contributed to their injury, this fact would not prevent them from recovering damages from a negligent teacher. But the older the student, the more likely the law will treat that individual as responsible for his or her own health and safety. Liability thus may depend on the age of the injured student.

Do Comparative Negligence Laws Make a Difference?

Yes. The most significant factor allowing negligent students to recover damages has been the trend toward adopting *comparative negligence* statutes, which now exist in a majority of states. Such laws permit judges or juries to compare the relative negligence of a plaintiff and a defendant in causing an injury and to reduce an award to the plaintiff in proportion to his or her negligence. For instance, in one Louisiana case where a 9-year-old jumped off a merry-go-round, thus sustaining injuries, the court awarded a 50 percent recovery upon finding that the student and school board were equally responsible for the injury.[11]

When Does a Student Assume the Risk of Being Injured?

The doctrine of *assumption of risk* is another defense against liability, particularly in competitive sports. It is based on the theory that people who appreciate the danger involved in an activity and still choose to do it expose themselves to certain predictable risks. When a 13-year-old girl's family sued the sponsor of a Catholic softball league due to serious injuries sustained during a softball game when she slid into a base, the court rejected a claim of "negligent instruction and training" of the coaches and officials, finding that the child was old enough to understand the inherent dangers of softball.[12] Similarly, where a 15-year-old high school student sneaked out of school with a family member who later sexually assaulted her at his home during the school day, the court found that the student had assumed the risk of harm even though she was too young to consent to sex.[13]

Can Teachers Assert Governmental Immunity as a Defense against Negligence?

No. *Governmental immunity* is a theory by which states and their agencies assert that because they are "sovereign" (like the English kings, from which this concept derived), they cannot be sued without their consent and should not be held liable for the negligence of their employees. In most states, the law "waives" such immunity up to a certain amount per occurrence, such as $100,000 in Maryland. In other states, the courts and legislatures have found that the purchase of liability insurance eliminates the defense altogether. Even in states where this doctrine can still prevent negligence suits against school districts, students may sue individual teachers, who may be found personally liable for their negligence in some instances.

Do Teachers Need to Purchase Professional Liability Insurance?

This is not necessary for most public school teachers. This is because teachers' unions usually provide liability insurance for their members as part of their union dues. The National Education Association, for example, provides all of its members with $1,000,000 liability insurance. In addition, the insurer will investigate, defend, and settle claims, even if they are groundless. Furthermore, most state laws provide that teachers are entitled to insurance coverage and defense counsel paid for by the school district, provided they are sued for actions committed within the scope of their employment and without malice.

Does the NCLB Protect Teachers from Liability?

Yes. The 2002 No Child Left Behind Act contains a provision known as the Paul D. Coverdell Teacher Protection Act, which immunizes from liability any teacher or administrator whose actions "were carried out in . . . furtherance of efforts to control, discipline, expel, or suspend a student or maintain order or control in the classroom or school."[14] This law prevents teachers from being liable for damages "in an action brought for harm based on the act or omission of a teacher acting within the scope of the teacher's employment" unless the teacher's act or omission clearly constitutes "willful or criminal misconduct."

Does a Waiver or Release Prevent an Injured Student from Suing?

Generally not. Most courts that have addressed the issue have found that such releases are invalid on public policy grounds. For example, the Washington Supreme Court held that school districts could not require parents to sign forms absolving the school of liability for sports accidents. Because athletics are "part and parcel" of the educational program, the court stated, the district is obligated to share in the risk of the dangers inherent in such programs.[15] Other courts have held that minors are not bound by releases executed by their parents.

Even where releases are not illegal, judges strictly construe such agreements. However, in recent years a few courts have upheld well-crafted releases, especially for students who voluntarily participate in athletic events, even when students sustain serious sport-related injuries. In one Massachusetts case, the court held that by requesting detailed health information about the student-athlete, the school district placed parents of an injured cheerleader on notice of the risk of injury. In so ruling, the court recognized the public policy of upholding such releases in order to protect nonprofit and school athletic organizations from certain financial ruin.[16]

Other Types of Liability

Are Teachers Liable If They Fail to Report Child Abuse?

Yes. Every state requires that teachers, along with administrators and counselors, report known or suspected cases of child abuse or neglect, and those who fail to do so are subject to penalties under the law. Every state also protects reporting individuals by granting civil or criminal immunity from liability on account of their reports, even if inaccurate, provided that the reports were made in "good faith" or "without malice."

Can Schools Be Held Liable for Failure to Maintain a Safe Environment?

Yes. A number of courts have held that a special relationship exists between educators and students because students are required to attend school and their care is entrusted to school officials. Under this theory, the courts have held schools liable for student injuries that are reasonably foreseeable. For example, a Florida court held that a school district was liable when a high school student was attacked and beaten by other students on school premises. The student was beaten outside the cafeteria while using the phone after a junior varsity football practice. The court found that the school was negligent in not providing for any supervision of the cafeteria area and that student misbehavior was a foreseeable result of such a lack of supervision.[17]

Some courts have applied this theory to hold schools liable when students are injured by nonstudents, particularly in unsupervised areas of the school. Where the injuries to a student are not foreseeable, the school district will not be held liable, such as when a fight is instigated by a student when the school had no knowledge about the aggressor's behavior.

Under the No Child Left Behind Act, if students attend a "persistently dangerous" school or are the victim of a criminal attack in their school, they may transfer to a safer school. The definition of "persistently dangerous" is determined by each state, but is generally based on a predetermined number of incidents involving guns, knives, or other weapons, and/or violent incidents resulting in arrest.

Can Schools Be Held Liable for Educational Malpractice?

Probably not. Some students have brought legal actions alleging that schools should be held liable for negligent teaching that injures a student intellectually or psychologically, just as physicians and lawyers are liable for professional malpractice. Rarely have students prevailed, however, because (1) there are no clear standards to determine whether the school has been educationally negligent; (2) there is no way to determine that a teacher's poor teaching was the proximate cause of a student's failure to learn; and (3) it would impose too great a financial burden on schools to hold them accountable for every such failure. Moreover, there are simply too many extraneous factors that influence a child's ability or inability to learn effectively to hold the teacher responsible. Only where school officials act intentionally and maliciously in injuring a child by, for instance, providing false information regarding the child's learning disability, altering school records to cover up their actions, or demeaning the child, will a court allow recovery under a theory of "educational malpractice."[18]

Can Schools Be Held Liable for Negligent Hiring or Retention of Unfit Employees?

Yes. Under this theory, employers can be liable when they are negligent in hiring or retaining employees whom they know or should have known are unfit or dangerous, or who place others at unreasonable risk of harm. If, for instance, a school knowingly hires a sexual predator who commits a sex offense on a student, the school district may be liable for negligent hiring and retention of the employee, particularly if the law requires prescreening of applicants to ensure that no such individuals are employed.

Can Schools Be Held Liable for Negligence When Teachers Are Injured?

Yes, but usually teachers are barred from suing their employers because of the availability of remedies under state laws offering workers' compensation to employees. Workers' compensation remedies, which include reimbursement of medical expenses and lost wages, tend to be the sole source of relief when teachers are injured on the job.

Can Parents Be Held Liable When Teachers Are Injured by Students?

Yes, where parents contributed to the student's dangerous behavior, as in the Wisconsin case of a child whose parents removed him from medication without informing the school, only to have the child violently injure a teacher.[19] Where parents do not have any knowledge of a child's propensity to engage in injurious conduct, they usually will not be held liable.

Can School Districts and School Officials Be Held Liable for Violating a Student's Constitutional Rights?

Yes. Public school officials who violate students' constitutional rights, such as free speech and expression, religious freedom, or the right to due process and equal protection of the laws, can be liable for damages under a federal statute referred to as "Section 1983," which allows suits against any person who, "under color of any statute, ordinance, regulation, custom or usage of any State . . . subjects, or causes to be subjected, any citizen of the United States . . . to the deprivation of any rights, privileges, or immunities secured by the Constitution" and laws.[20]

The U.S. Supreme Court has ruled that most school districts, like other local governments, are "persons" and can be held liable under Section 1983 for violations of students' and teachers' constitutional rights, but only if the violations are the result of a school district's official policy, practice, or custom that shows deliberate indifference to an individual's constitutional rights. Generally, there must be evidence of a pattern of indifference and even hostility toward students' constitutional rights before the courts find a violation of Section 1983, as occurred when school administrators turned a blind eye to a student who was mercilessly taunted and beaten by his fellow students for being a homosexual.[21]

School officials such as board members and administrators acting under color of state law can also be held liable under Section 1983, but may be entitled to assert a *qualified immunity* (and thus avoid liability for money damages) unless they "knew or reasonably should have known that the action they took within their sphere of official responsibility would violate the constitutional rights of the students affected."[22] Thus, school officials are protected for good-faith actions taken to fulfill their official duties, such as maintaining order and protecting student safety. A 1982 Supreme Court decision held that public officials "generally are shielded from liability for civil damages insofar as their conduct does not violate clearly established statutory or constitutional rights of which a reasonable person would have known."[23] To decide what constitutes "clearly established" law capable of supporting a finding of liability by a public official such as a teacher or principal for violating an individual's constitutional rights, the courts decide whether prior cases placed the public employee on notice that his or her conduct violated constitutional rights.

To minimize the risk of personal liability, school board members, administrators, and teachers should monitor federal constitutional decisions to remain aware of what is expected of them. Regular updates of legal developments obtained from school board attorneys can prevent otherwise costly litigation.

Can School Officials or Teachers Be Held Liable under Section 1983 for Abuse of Students by Teachers or Other Students?

Rarely. The courts require that a "special relationship" exist between the plaintiff and the government official to find such liability. An example where such liability is likely is when a teacher or administrator was deliberately indifferent toward known, escalating violence directed at a student.

Several courts have found that public school students have a constitutionally protected interest to be free from violations of bodily integrity by school employees, thus placing teachers and principals at risk of constitutional liability when, for instance, they slap or sexually abuse students. In one case, a court stated that "no reasonable principal could think it constitutional to intentionally punch, slap, grab, and slam students into lockers."[24] But the majority of courts require a pattern of indifference by school officials tantamount to an unwritten school policy before imposing such liability on school boards for the acts of individual teachers. Even less likely is a finding of such liability when the harm is caused by fellow students, since courts do not tend to hold school officials responsible for the acts of third parties over whom they have little or no control. One exception is a 1996 case in which a gay male student suffered ongoing harassment and in-school violence by fellow students to which school officials turned a blind eye. The court found that school officials were liable for discriminating against the student on the basis of his sexual orientation, a violation of the equal protection clause of the Fourteenth Amendment. The court also found that homosexuals are a "defined minority" protected from discrimination both under the Constitution and state law, and that the student was treated differently based on his sexual orientation when school officials permitted others to assault him.[25]

Damages and Defamation

What Kinds of Damages Are Awarded by the Courts?

Courts can award several kinds of damages, the most common of which is for *compensatory* losses, such as medical and therapy costs, lost wages, and other expenses incurred due to the negligence or other liability attributed to school officials. *Exemplary* or *punitive* damages may be awarded where defendants have shown malice, fraud, or reckless disregard for an injured person's safety or constitutional rights. The purpose of such damages is to deter future violations by the defendants and others. *Nominal damages,* like $1.00, are awarded when a plaintiff has been wronged but has been unable to show actual damages.

When students or teachers succeed in proving a violation of their civil or constitutional rights, courts are empowered to award attorneys' fees incurred in proving their case. Often such fees exceed the actual value of the verdict.

What Constitutes Libel and Slander?

Making a false statement that hurts another person's reputation can be one of two forms of defamation of character: *libel* is the written form, whereas *slander* is verbal. Statements are defamatory if they tend to expose another person to hatred, shame, disgrace, contempt, or ridicule. To be actionable, defamatory statements must be communicated to third parties. For example, if a principal writes a defamatory letter to a teacher, no libel is involved unless the principal shares it with someone besides the teacher.

Is Truth a Defense to a Defamation Action?

Usually, although in some states it is not enough to avoid liability where the defamation was published with a "malicious motive," or where there is lack of a "justifiable purpose" to support the communication in the first place.

What Kinds of Statements Are Defamatory?

Some statements are automatically assumed to be defamatory, such as: (1) imputing a criminal offense; (2) imputing a loathsome disease (e.g., a sexually transmitted disease); (3) disparaging professional competency; or (4) imputing a lack of chastity or morality (e.g., a charge of child abuse). Other statements can be defamatory, but require additional proof that they, in fact, injured someone's reputation.

When Can Defamatory Statements Be Made and Still Avoid Liability?

Statements that are clearly understood as being satirical or humorous and that are not understood to state actual facts about a person (as, for instance, in an editorial that merely offers an *opinion*) are not defamatory. Thus, a yearbook containing a teacher's picture accompanied by a caption suggesting that the teacher was involved in a sexual relationship with another teacher was not found to be defamatory, because it was clearly intended to be humorous.[26]

What Kinds of Statements about Teachers Have Been Found to Be Defamatory on Their Face?

The courts have found the following statements disparaging and thus actionable libel or slander: (1) "He is not a fit person to teach in any school. He is no good as a teacher. . . . [H]e [sleeps in class]";[27] (2) a statement before the school board that a teacher was "intoxicated at the public dinner";[28] (3) a newspaper article accusing a teacher of killing a child;[29] and (4) a television report accusing a teacher of directing other students to assault another student.[30]

Recently a Colorado court concluded that since homosexual relationships were no longer illegal in that state, false statements accusing a teacher of being a homosexual could no longer be deemed actionable slander.[31]

Can Teachers Sue Their Superiors for Defamatory Statements Made in Evaluations, Recommendation Letters, or Other Work-Related Communications?

Not easily. Supervisors, such as principals and other administrators, generally have a *qualified privilege* to comment on matters concerning the operation of the schools. Under this privilege school administrators are not liable for defamatory statements, even if false, if they are under a duty to comment on the quality of a teacher's performance and act in good faith. This privilege extends to comments made in letters of recommendation by teachers as well as administrators and, in many states, such letters are protected from being deemed defamatory, even if false, provided they are not made maliciously.

Can Students Sue Teachers for Written Statements in Students' Files?

Not easily. As in the employment context described previously, they are entitled to a *qualified privilege* if comments contained in student records are made in good faith, even if false.

However, if a teacher knowingly spreads false gossip that harms a student's reputation, for instance in the teachers' lounge or classroom, the teacher may be liable for slander. But a teacher's statements may be conditionally privileged if they are made as part of the disciplinary process or of the teacher's administrative responsibilities. Similarly, a teacher who provides a negative letter of reference, if not made in bad faith or maliciously, is protected from liability for libel.

Finally, a teacher may not be liable for defamation because of a poor grade given to a student, because the courts refuse to interfere with the authority of educational authorities in determining grades.

Do Any Constitutional Considerations Apply in Slander or Libel Cases?

Yes. In *New York Times Co. v. Sullivan,* the U.S. Supreme Court ruled that the First Amendment's guarantees of freedom of speech and press bar public officials from being awarded damages for libel or slander unless they can prove that such statements were made with actual malice.[32] "Actual malice" means that the defendant made the libelous or slanderous statements either knowing they were false or with a reckless disregard for the truth of the statements. In short, where public officials are concerned, there is a far higher burden of proof before establishing defamation.

Courts have applied this rule to school board members, superintendents, and even high school principals.[33] Most courts have tended to exclude teachers from the definition of "public officials" because of their more remote relationship with the conduct of government.

Does the *New York Times* Standard Apply to Statements of Opinion as Well as of Fact?

Yes, according to a 1990 U.S. Supreme Court decision,[34] in which a high school wrestling coach sued a newspaper after it published an editorial stating that the coach had "apparently" lied under oath in a judicial proceeding. The newspaper argued that this statement was not fact, but purely an opinion and therefore not subject to a libel lawsuit. The Court carefully distinguished between pure "opinion" and opinions that imply an association of objective fact, which could be deemed defamatory. Thus, the Court concluded that reasonable readers could conclude that the newspaper was accusing the coach of perjury, and thus it had libeled him.

Child Abuse and Neglect: The Duty to Report and Liability of Schools and Teachers

What Is Child Abuse?

Though the definition of "child abuse" varies from state to state, the National Committee for Prevention of Child Abuse defines it as a nonaccidental injury to a child for which there is no "reasonable" explanation. Federal law defines child abuse and neglect as "physical or mental injury, sexual abuse or exploitation, negligent treatment, or maltreatment of a child under the age of eighteen . . . by a person who is responsible for the child's welfare, under circumstances which indicate that the child's health or welfare is harmed or threatened thereby."[35] Because child abuse is a state, rather than federal crime, the foregoing definition is contained in legislation intended to provide federal aid to local agencies concerned with child abuse. Although state laws vary, they all use a combination of two or more of the following elements in defining abuse and neglect: (1) physical injury; (2) mental or emotional injury; and (3) sexual molestation or exploitation.

Is Distinguishing between Abuse and Neglect Important?

No. States require educators to report both types of mistreatment of youngsters.

Must Child Abuse and Neglect Be Reported?

Yes, in every state. In most states, school officials must report suspected child abuse and neglect to law enforcement or child protective services authorities, and may not conduct their own internal investigation of such alleged abuse, even if the suspected abuser is a school system employee, until after law enforcement or child protective authorities have completed their investigation and made decisions regarding prosecution.

Do Laws Require Educators to Report Child Abuse and Neglect?

Yes. Some state statutes explicitly name "school counselors" among the mandatory reporters of child abuse or neglect. Others include among them "educators," "other school personnel," or "employees or officials of any public or private school." Still others require "any person" who works with children and has "reasonable cause to believe" that abuse or neglect is occurring to make a report. Such general requirements include teachers, therapists, and counselors who work with children.

Even if a superior fails or refuses to report an alleged act of child abuse or neglect once reported by a teacher, a teacher is still obligated to report it to law enforcement or child protective services officials. In some states, failure to report suspected child abuse is grounds for termination of tenured teachers. Allegations of child abuse are serious because they can cause irreparable damage to an individual's reputation and career. In one Maryland case, students who admitted falsely accusing their teacher of sexual abuse were found liable for significant damages, even though the teacher had access to an administrative appeal process meant to vindicate his reputation and restore his job.[36]

Can Educators Be Registered as Suspected Child Abusers?

Yes, in states which require that a register of cases be maintained. At times, inconsistencies exist between the disciplinary policies and practices of a school and the criteria used by social services agencies as to what is excessive punishment sufficient to constitute child abuse. In one Arkansas case, an assistant principal who paddled a child pursuant to that state's corporal punishment law was not placed on the child abuse registry because there was no proof of excessive violence.[37]

Because placement on a child abuse registry for a number of years carries a serious stigma, it is deemed to implicate a teacher's "liberty interest" protected by the Fourteenth Amendment. Thus, teachers have the right to a hearing and to insist on proof by a *preponderance of the evidence,* not merely *credible evidence.*

Is the Reporter of Child Abuse or Neglect Protected from Lawsuits?

Yes. Every state provides immunity by law for civil suit and criminal prosecution that might arise from the reporting of suspected child abuse or neglect. Such immunity applies to all mandatory or permissible reporters who act in "good faith." In many states, good faith is presumed; therefore the person suing the reporter has the burden to prove that the reporter acted in bad faith. To be eligible for federal funds under the Child Abuse Prevention, Adoption and Family Services Act,[38] states must grant immunity to reporters. All states have complied with this requirement. The expressed intent of immunity legislation is to encourage reporting without fear of civil or criminal liability.

Should Counselors Violate Privileged Communication by Reporting Suspected Cases of Abuse or Neglect?

Yes. In fact they must. First, most states deny such privilege to counselors in any legal proceeding. Second, as a matter of public policy it is more important to require the reporting than to respect the privilege, as is the case with students who express an intent to commit violence against themselves or others. Finally, because counselors and teachers are among those who must report, *the legal requirement of reporting overrides any claim to privilege or confidential communication.*

Do Religious Beliefs Exempt One from Liability for Child Abuse?

Sometimes, as when, for instance, medical procedures are foregone for religious reasons. However, in those states courts have the power to override the wishes of parents in the interest of protecting the health and safety of their children.

Is There a Penalty for Failing to Report Child Abuse or Neglect?

Most states have both civil and criminal penalties, although they are generally predicated on proof that failure to report suspected child abuse or neglect was willful or knowing. It is this additional element that has resulted in an absence of any reported criminal proceedings against a teacher for failing to report suspected abuse.

Is a Social Services Agency Liable for Failure to Protect a Child after Abuse Has Been Reported?

No. The Supreme Court held in 1989 that state social services officials could not be liable for the beating of a child by his father after having returned him to the family home despite a history of previous violent behavior in that home. Although the Supreme Court acknowledged the tragic facts of the case and the fact that the social service worker was aware of the brutality of previous beatings suffered by the child, a majority of the Court ruled that courts cannot impose liability on government agencies for the violent behavior of third parties.[39]

Guidelines

- In order to be found liable for a student's injury, the student must prove that the teacher (or other responsible individual in the school setting) owed a duty of care to the student, the teacher breached that duty, and the breach (either through action or inaction) was the cause of the student's injury, causing provable damages.

- School officials can be held personally liable for damages if they violate clearly established constitutional rights of students or teachers.

- Damages awardable for negligence or other forms of liability include compensatory damages for actual out-of-pocket losses, such as medical and therapy bills, as well as punitive damages intended to punish and deter future actionable conduct.

- Victims of defamatory statements, that is, comments that impugn their honesty, integrity, or reputation, have the right to sue for slander (where the defamation is verbal) or libel (where it is written).

- Defamatory comments about public officials, such as school board members, superintendents, and in some states school principals, are subject to a higher standard of proof, due to constitutional free speech considerations. Thus, under the principles of *New York Times Co. v. Sullivan,* the defamatory comments must have been knowingly false or in reckless disregard of the truth.

- Negative comments about teachers made by supervisors in the course of evaluating performance are generally subject to a *qualified privilege,* which protects supervisors from liability unless teachers show that the comments were made maliciously or in bad faith.

- Teachers are protected from liability where, in good faith, they give a student a poor grade or negative reference.

- All states require teachers to report suspected child abuse or neglect to the proper law enforcement or child protective service authorities. Failure to do so may subject teachers to civil or criminal liability, and in some states, is grounds for termination even of tenured teachers.

- Even if a teacher's report of suspected child abuse proves to be unfounded, so long as the report was made in good faith, the teacher is entitled to immunity from liability.

Notes

1. *Eisel v. Bd. of Educ. of Montgomery Cnty.*, 597 A.2d 447 (Md. 1991).
2. *Sheehan v. St. Peter's Catholic Sch.*, 188 N.W.2d 868 (Minn. 1971).
3. *Bartell v. Palos Verdes Peninsula Sch. Dist.*, 83 Cal. App. 3d 492 (1978).
4. *Carrol K. v. Fayette Co. Bd. of Educ.*, 19 F.Supp. 2d 618 (S.D.W. Va. 1998).
5. *Oast v. Lafayette Parish Sch. Bd.*, 591 So.2d 1257 (La. 1991).
6. *Allen v. Crawford*, 438 S.E.2d 178 (Ga. App. 1993).
7. *Nash v. Rapides Parish Sch. Bd.*, 188 So.2d 508 (La. App. 1966).
8. *Kaufman v. City of New York*, 214 N.Y.S.2d 767 (N.Y. Sup. Ct. 1961).
9. *Collins v. Sch. Bd. of Broward Co.*, 471 So.2d 560 (Fla. App. 1985).
10. *Miles v. Sch. Dist. No. 138 of Cheyenne Co.*, 281 N.W.2d 396 (Neb. 1979).
11. *Rollins v. Concordia Parish Sch. Bd.*, 465 So.2d 213 (La. App. 1985).
12. *Kelly v. McCarrick*, 841 A.2d 869 (2004).
13. *Tate v. Bd. of Educ. of Prince George's Co.*, 843 A.2d 890 (2003).
14. 20 U.S.C. § 6736(a).
15. *Wagenblast v. Odessa Sch. Dist.*, 758 P.2d 968 (Wash. 1988).
16. *Sharon v. City of Newton*, 769 N.E.2d 738 (2002).
17. *Broward Co. Sch. Bd. v. Ruiz*, 493 So.2d 474 (Fla. App. 1986).
18. *Hunter v. Bd. of Educ. of Montgomery Cnty.*, 425 A.2d 681 (Md. Ct. Spec. App. 1981).
19. *Nieuwendorp v. Am. Family Ins.*, 529 N.W.2d 594 (Wis. 1995).
20. 42 U.S.C. § 1983.
21. *Flores v. Morgan Hill Unified Sch. Dist.*, 324 F.3d 1130 (9th Cir. 2003).
22. *Wood v. Strickland*, 420 U.S. 308 (1975).
23. *Harlow v. Fitzgerald*, 457 U.S. 800 (1982).
24. *P.B. v. Koch*, 96 F.3d 1298 (9th Cir. 1996).
25. *Nabozny v. Podlesny*, 92 F.3d 446 (7th Cir. 1996).
26. *Salek v. Passaic Collegiate Sch.*, 605 A.2d 276 (1992).
27. *Mulcaby v. Deitrick*, 176 N.E. 481 (Ohio Ct. App. 1931).
28. *Ford v. Jeane*, 106 So. 588 (La. 1925).
29. *Doan v. Kelley*, 23 N.E. 266 (1890).
30. *Snitowski v. WMAQ-TV*, 696 N.E. 2d 761 (Ill. App. 1 Dist. 1998).
31. *Hayes v. Smith*, 832 P. 2d 1022 (Colo. Ct. App. 1991).
32. 376 U.S. 254 (1964).
33. *Kapiloff v. Dunn*, 343 A.2d 251 (1975).
34. *Milkovich v. Lorain Journal Co.*, 497 U.S. 1 (1990).
35. National Child Abuse Prevention and Treatment Act of 1974, 42 U.S.C. § 5201 *et seq.*
36. *Reichardt v. Flynn*, 374 823 A.2d 566 (2003).
37. *Ark. Dep't. of Human Servs. v. Caldwell*, 832 S.W.2d 510 (Ark. Ct. App. 1992).
38. 42 U.S.C. § 5116 *et seq.*
39. *DeShaney v. Winnebago Cnty. Dep't. of Soc. Svcs.*, 489 U.S. 189 (1989).

chapter 4

Teacher Freedom of Expression

Academic Freedom, Association, Appearance, and Copyright

The U.S. Supreme Court has ruled that public school teachers have a right to freedom of expression. However, no right is absolute. Therefore, this chapter examines the scope and limits of teachers' freedom of speech in and out of school, freedom of association, how they can protect their creative expression, and when schools can regulate educators' personal appearance.

Controversial Expression Out of Class

Can Teachers Criticize School Policy? The Pickering Case

Marvin Pickering was an Illinois high school teacher who published a sarcastic letter in the local newspaper criticizing the way his superintendent and school board
raised and spent school funds and the "totalitarianism teachers live in." Angered by
the letter,'the board fired Pickering because the letter contained false statements,
"damaged the professional reputations" of administrators, and was "detrimental
to the . . . administration of the schools." Pickering argued that his letter should be
protected by his right to free speech, and the U.S. Supreme Court agreed.

      The Court found that Pickering's criticism of the way administrators raised
and allocated funds was not directed toward people Pickering normally worked
with and raised no question of student discipline or harmony with coworkers.
Therefore, the Court "unequivocally" rejected the board's position that critical
public comments by a teacher on matters of public concern may be grounds for
dismissal. On the contrary, because teachers are likely to have informed opinions
about how school funds should be spent, "it is essential that they be able to speak
out freely on such questions without fear of retaliatory dismissal."[1]

Could Pickering Be Fired If His Statements Were Not Accurate?

Not in this case, because his incorrect statements were not intentional and did not
impede his teaching or interfere with the operation of the school. Therefore, the
Court concluded that "absent proof of false statements knowingly or recklessly
made by him, a teacher's exercise of his right to speak on issues of public importance may not furnish the basis for his dismissal."

Can Teachers Ever Be Disciplined for Publicizing Their Views or Criticizing Immediate Superiors?

Yes. According to the Pickering decision, there are some positions in education
"in which the need for confidentiality is so great that even completely correct
public statements" might be grounds for dismissal. For example, a judge upheld
the punishment of a guidance counselor for unprofessional disclosures of confidential information about a student's sexual orientation. In addition, some public
criticism of an immediate superior by a teacher that seriously undermined their
working relationship might justify appropriate discipline. On the other hand, a
court protected a Texas teacher who testified before the Dallas School Board
about the inability of his principal and coworkers to deal with "multiracial student

bodies." The judge ruled that, in this case, "society's interest in information concerning the operation of its schools outweighs any strain on the teacher-principal relationship."[2] Furthermore, teachers cannot be punished for communicating directly with their school board about matters of public concern rather than going through the chain of command.

Is Private Criticism Protected?

It depends on the circumstances. The Supreme Court has extended the *Pickering* ruling to apply to private as well as public criticism, and it protected a teacher who complained to her principal about her school's racially discriminatory practices. However, a court upheld the dismissal of a teacher who told her black principal, "I hate all black folks." In this case, the school's interest in employing effective educators outweighed the teacher's free speech interests.[3] Concerning confrontations between teachers and immediate superiors, judges consider the time, place, and manner of the confrontation when balancing the rights in conflict.

Are Teachers' Personal Complaints Protected by the First Amendment?

No. According to the Supreme Court, "when a public employee speaks not as a citizen upon matters of public concern, but instead as an employee upon matters only of personal interest" courts will not review the public agency's disciplinary decision.[4] In Illinois, for example, a court wrote that a series of "unprofessional and insulting" memoranda to school officials were not protected because the teacher was not speaking as a citizen concerned with educational problems but was expressing "his own private disagreement" about policies he refused to follow.[5] Similarly, a court did not protect a teacher's letters that complained about overcrowding in her classroom which she claimed was a safety hazard. The court explained that, if the reason for the letters were a personal grievance, a passing reference to safety will not transform a personal problem into a matter of public concern.[6]

When Are Teachers' Statements Protected as Matters of Public Concern?

According to the Supreme Court, when they relate to "any matter of political, social, or other concern to the community."[7] It also may depend on the statement's content, form, and context. For example, a judge protected a Chicago teacher who was disciplined for criticizing her school's kindergarten program, which she claimed violated state standards. Since she presented her concerns and an alternative plan to parents and the school council as well as her principal, the judge ruled that her discussion of the program "was truly a protected matter of public concern, not simply an unprotected complaint about her employment."[8]

If a Teacher's Statements Are about Public Concerns, Are They Always Protected?

No. If a teacher's controversial statements are a matter of public concern, then judges will balance the teacher's right to discuss issues of public interest against the school's interest in efficiency. In a Rhode Island case, for example, the court ruled that the right of a teacher to videotape health and safety hazards in her high school outweighed the administration's concern that the videotape would have a negative effect on the school's reputation. According to the judge, First Amendment rights cannot be conditioned on whether the image of the school is adversely affected. Otherwise, wrote the court, a teacher's free speech rights would almost always be denied since a school administrator "rarely challenges an employee's right to speak where the speech is complimentary."[9]

On the other hand, teachers' public comments are not protected when judges consider the manner, content, and consequences of the expression and conclude that the school's interest outweighs the teacher's. This occurred when a Chicago teacher was fired for publishing several standardized, copyrighted tests to stir debate about the testing. According to the judge, the admirable goal of increasing discussion about standardized tests "fails to convert [the teacher's] copyright violations to conduct protected by the First Amendment." Thus, the school's interest in promoting its educational mission outweighed the teacher's interest in criticizing the tests by publishing them.[10]

Do Whistle-Blower Laws Protect Teachers?

Yes. All 50 states have whistle-blower protection statutes. Generally they supplement the First Amendment by protecting public employees who in good faith report a violation of law. Many also cover gross waste of public funds or specific dangers to health or safety. The laws also include remedies for whistle-blowers who suffer reprisals.

Are Teachers at Private Schools That Receive State Funds Protected by the First Amendment?

No. The First Amendment only protects teachers at public schools. For example, even if a private school for special education students receives most or even all of

. . . . •

55

its funds from public school districts, teachers at those schools can be dismissed for publicly opposing their school's policies.

Academic Freedom

What Is Academic Freedom?

Academic freedom includes the right of teachers to speak freely about their subject, to raise questions about traditional values and beliefs, and to select appropriate teaching materials and methods. While judges have protected academic freedom among public university professors, recent decisions have limited academic freedom among elementary and secondary teachers and have balanced it against competing educational values.

Does Academic Freedom Protect the Use of Controversial Materials?

Earlier cases ruled that it does *if* the material is relevant to the subject, appropriate to the age and maturity of the students, and does not cause disruption. Thus, a 1969 decision upheld the right of English teacher Robert Keefe to assign a scholarly article from the *Atlantic Monthly* magazine that contained the word *motherfucker* and offended parents but not the high school seniors. According to the judge, the sensibilities of offended parents "are not the full measure of what is proper in education."[11] But, even this liberal decision did not suggest that teachers have a right to use any language in class. According to the court, whether offensive language is protected would depend on the specific situation—the students, the subject, the word used, the purpose of its use, and whether it has been prohibited. Since there is no Supreme Court decision on academic freedom in public schools, court decisions vary, and the trend of recent cases is to narrow and limit such freedom.

Can a School Board Require or Prohibit Specific Texts?

Yes. School boards usually have authority to select or eliminate texts, even if teachers disagree. In Colorado, for example, teachers challenged a board decision banning 10 books from an approved list for use in elective literature courses. The court noted that teachers could not be prohibited from mentioning and briefly discussing the books. But the judge explained that state laws give local school boards substantial control over the curriculum, including authority to add or eliminate courses and the books that are assigned.

Similarly, an appeals court upheld the authority of a Florida board to remove Chaucer's *The Miller's Tale* and Aristophanes' *Lysistrata* from the curriculum because of their "sexual explicitness." The case illustrates the difference between what courts and school boards think is lawful and wise. While the judges ruled that the board's decision was not unconstitutional, they emphasized that they did "not endorse the board's decision" and "seriously questioned" how these "masterpieces" could harm high school students.[12]

Can School Boards Remove Library Books for Any Reasons?

No. A board's discretion to remove books must be used in a constitutional manner, and decisions cannot be based on a desire to promote a particular political or religious view. Although library books can be removed if they are not relevant or appropriate for the age and grade of the students, the Supreme Court has ruled that "boards may not remove books from school library shelves simply because they dislike the ideas contained in those books."[13]

Can Social Studies Teachers Be Prohibited from Discussing Controversial Issues?

It would probably be unconstitutional for administrators to order teachers of history, civics, or current events not to discuss controversial questions. This was the ruling in a Texas case involving a civics teacher's unit on race relations and his response to a question stating that he didn't oppose interracial marriage. When parents complained, the principal told the teacher to not discuss controversial issues. After the teacher replied that it was impossible to avoid controversy in a current events class, he was fired for insubordination. The judge noted that teachers have a duty to be "objective in presenting [their] personally held opinions" and to ensure that differing views are presented. In this case, however, the court ruled that the teacher acted professionally and did not subject students to indoctrination.[14] On the other hand, teachers have no right to use the classroom to preach about their religious or political views.

Does Academic Freedom Allow Teachers to Disregard a Text or Curriculum?

No. Thus, a court held that a history teacher had no right to substitute his own reading list for the school's official list. As the judge noted, "The First Amendment has never required school districts to abdicate control over public school curricula."[15] And, in a California case where a biology teacher objected to teaching evolution, a judge wrote: "If every teacher . . . omitted those topics which are different from beliefs they hold, a curriculum . . . would be useless."[16]

Can Teachers Be Punished for Discussing Topics That Are Not Relevant?

Yes. Academic freedom does not protect materials, discussions, or comments that are not relevant to the assigned subject. Thus, a court upheld the dismissal of three 8th-grade teachers for distributing movie brochures ("to promote rapport") that included positive views on drugs, that had no relation to the curriculum, and that promoted views that were contrary to the requirement that students be taught the "harmful effects of narcotics."[17]

Can a Teacher Be Punished for Showing an R-Rated Film?

Probably, although it may depend on the students and the movie. An example of how not to do it was provided by Jacqueline Fowler, who showed the R-rated film, *Pink Floyd—The Wall,* at the request of her high school students while she completed her grade cards. She had not seen the film but asked a student to "edit out" any parts that were unsuitable by holding an 8½ × 11-inch file folder in front of the 25-inch screen. Even if the film included valuable messages, the judge ruled that it was not constitutionally protected. By introducing a "sexually explicit movie into a classroom of adolescents without preview, preparation or discussion," the judge wrote, Fowler "abdicated her function as an educator" and demonstrated a "blatant lack of judgment."[18]

Is a Teacher's Offensive Out-of-Class Language Protected?

It might be if the language does not damage his or her effectiveness as a teacher. On the other hand, a court upheld the dismissal of a teacher for distributing copies of racist "jokes" in school to a coworker that contained "vicious" statements against African Americans and "disregarded standards of behavior the school had a right to expect."[19]

Teaching Methods

Can a Teacher Be Punished for Using a Controversial Method?

Not usually, unless the teaching method is clearly prohibited. If a teacher does not know that the method is prohibited, it would probably be a violation of due process to punish a teacher for using that method unless it had no recognized educational purpose.

In discussing the subject of taboo words, English teacher Roger Mailloux wrote the word *fuck* on the blackboard and asked his 11th-grade class for an explanation. After a student volunteered the word meant sexual intercourse, Mailloux said: "We have two words, sexual intercourse, and this word on the board; one is accepted by society, the other is not accepted. It is a taboo word."[20]

As a result of this incident, Mailloux was fired and took his case to court. The judge found that the word *fuck* was relevant to the topic of taboo words, that Mailloux's method did not disturb the students, and that educational experts were in conflict about whether it was appropriate to use the controversial word in class. Since teachers should not be required to "guess what conduct or utterance may lose him his position" and since Mailloux did not know that his method was prohibited, the judge ruled that it was a violation of due process to fire him.

In a more recent case, a court explained that schools may restrict teaching methods if two conditions are met. First, the restriction must be related to "legitimate educational concerns." Second, schools must have notified the teacher about what conduct was prohibited. However, the court did not require schools to "expressly prohibit every imaginable inappropriate conduct."[21] Rather, the question is: Was it reasonable for the teacher to know his or her conduct was prohibited?

When Are Controversial Methods Not Protected?

Controversial methods are not protected by academic freedom when they are inappropriate for the age and maturity of the students, not supported by any significant professional opinion, or when they are prohibited by school policy. Thus, a court upheld the punishment of an English teacher who repeatedly used the words *penis* and *clitoris* and refused to de-emphasize the sexual aspects of the literary works he discussed in class.[22]

May a School Refuse to Rehire a Teacher Because of Disagreements over Teaching Methods or Philosophy?

Yes. When an English teacher was not rehired because she emphasized student choice and failed to cover the material she had been told to teach, she went to court, but lost. The issue, explained the judge, is not which educational approach has greater merit, but whether the school may require conformity to its philosophy and decline to rehire a teacher whose methods are not consistent with its educational goals.[23]

Is Academic Freedom the Same in Public Schools and Colleges?

No. In explaining why academic freedom is greater in colleges than in secondary schools, a judge wrote that the high school faculty does not have

> the broad discretion as to teaching methods, nor usually the intellectual qualifications of university professors. . . . While secondary schools are not rigid disciplinary institutions, neither are they open forums in which mature adults . . . exchange ideas on a level of parity. Moreover, a secondary school student, unlike most college students, is usually required to attend school classes and may have no choice as to his teachers.[24]

Freedom of Association

Is Freedom of Association a Constitutional Right?

Yes. Although freedom of association is not explicitly mentioned in the U.S. Constitution, the Supreme Court has held that the right is "implicit" in the freedoms of speech, assembly, and petition. "Among the rights protected by the First Amendment," wrote Justice Powell, "is the right of individuals to associate to further their personal beliefs."[25]

Can a Teacher Be Fired for Belonging to a Communist, Nazi, or Subversive Organization?

Not merely for being a member of such an organization. According to the Supreme Court, those who join a subversive organization but do not share its unlawful purposes and do not participate in its unlawful activities pose no threat, either as citizens or teachers.

Can a Teacher Be Dismissed for Being Active in an Organization That Promotes Sexual Relations between Men and Boys?

Yes, but not just because he was a member of the organization. Peter Melzer went to court when he was fired after a widely publicized video disclosed that he was an active member and writer for NAMBLA (the North American Man/Boy Love Association) that advocates legalizing consensual sexual relations between men and boys. Although there was no evidence that Melzer ever engaged in inappropriate conduct with students, the media attention led to intense conflict in the school community. Although the court acknowledged that the First Amendment protects the "association rights of an individual like Melzer, no matter how different, unpopular, or morally repugnant society may find his activities," it upheld his dismissal. The court explained that, in the context of teaching, "Melzer's activities strike such a sensitive chord that . . . the disruption they cause is great enough" to outweigh his freedom of association rights.[26]

Can Schools Refuse to Hire Teachers Because Their Children Attend Private School?

No. When an Ohio teacher was refused a teaching position because he did not send his son to a public school, he sued. In this 2004 case, the court ruled that parents have a constitutional right to send their children to private or public schools, and administrators can be held liable when the only reason for denying teachers employment is because they enrolled their children in a private school.[27]

Can Students Attend Schools Where Their Parents Teach?

Generally, this is permitted, but many school districts prohibit students from being assigned to classes taught by their own parents. Some teacher union contracts, however, include as a fringe benefit the right of teachers to have their children attend their same school even if they live outside that school's geographic boundaries.

Can a Teacher Be Prohibited from Marrying an Administrator?

Yes. Or an administrator could be transferred or dismissed for marrying a teacher. Schools can justify such actions to avoid conflicts of interest. Thus, a court ruled in favor of a Minnesota board that did not renew a principal's contract when he married the physical education teacher in violation of board policy.[28] Similarly, a New York court upheld the transfer of a teacher who married an assistant principal who supervised her. The court supported the district policy prohibiting any employee supervising a "near relative," to avoid the "perception of favoritism on the part of other members of the teaching faculty."[29]

Can Spouses Be Prohibited from Teaching in the Same School?

Yes, according to a ruling by a federal appeals court that upheld an antinepotism policy prohibiting spouses from working on the same campus.

Can Teachers Be Prohibited from Intimate Associations with Students after They Graduate?

Yes, if schools wish to have such a prohibition. For example, a 2004 federal decision upheld the dismissal of a Michigan teacher who had a sexual relationship with a student after her graduation. According to the court, schools can act "prophylactically" by prohibiting such a relationship with former students "within a year or two" of graduation to prevent students from being perceived as "prospects eligible for dating" soon after they graduate.[30]

Can Teachers Wear Political Buttons or Symbols to Class?

Yes, as long as such symbols do not interfere with a teacher's classroom performance and are not an attempt to proselytize or indoctrinate students. On the other hand, teachers can be prohibited from promoting political candidates in class and can be disciplined for doing so.

Can a Teacher Be Prohibited from Being a School Board Member?

Yes. To prevent conflicts of interest, teachers can be prohibited from serving on school boards in districts where they work.

Can a Teacher Be Prohibited from Running for a Political Office?

State laws and district policies differ, and courts are split on this issue. Some hold that it is reasonable to require a teacher to resign before campaigning for public office. On the other hand, an Oregon court ruled that a law prohibiting public employees from running for *any* office is unconstitutional—particularly if the office is part-time or nonpartisan.

While school boards can protect their educational system from undue political activity that substantially interferes with their schools, prohibiting teachers from engaging in any political activity goes too far, violates a teacher's constitutional rights, and deprives the community of the political participation of its teachers.

Personal Appearance

Do Teachers Have a Constitutional Right to Wear Beards or Long Hair?

Probably not. When an Illinois math teacher's contract was not renewed because of his beard, he went to court. The judge wrote that hairstyle was of "relatively trivial importance" when judging a teacher's qualifications and that a teacher could "explain the Pythagorean theorem as well in a T-shirt as in a three-piece suit." However, he ruled that grooming choices were not protected by the Constitution and that, if a school board decided a "teacher's style of dress and plumage" had a negative impact on education, the interest of the teacher is subordinate to the interest of the school.[31]

Do Teachers Have a Right to Dress as They Wish?

No. Therefore, teachers who challenge clothing regulations rarely claim they can dress anyway they wish; rather, they might argue that the dress code is arbitrary, unreasonable, or discriminatory. This was the argument of a tenured Louisiana teacher who was suspended for violating a policy requiring male teachers to wear neckties. Since the purpose of the rule was to enhance the professional image of teachers in the eyes of students and parents, the court did not find the policy arbitrary or unreasonable.[32]

Can a Teacher Be Punished without Due Process for Violating a School's Grooming Code?

No. This was the ruling in the case of David Lucia, who grew a beard in violation of an unwritten school policy. When he failed to shave his beard after meeting with the superintendent and school committee, he was suspended for "insubordination and improper example," and he was not invited to a meeting at which the committee dismissed him. A court ruled that the committee violated Lucia's due process rights since, prior to his case, there was no announced policy against teachers wearing beards, and the committee did not explain that failure to remove his beard would result in dismissal.[33]

This case indicates that teachers cannot be dismissed for violating a school's dress or grooming policy unless (1) teachers are given adequate notice of the policy and the consequences of not following it; and (2) they have the right to a hearing if facts are in dispute.

Copyright Law: Protecting Creative Expression and Fair Use

The purpose of copyrights is to protect the creative works of authors and to prevent others from using them without the author's permission. The federal Copyright Act of 1976 gives authors control over the reproduction and distribution of their work and enables a copyright owner to sue anyone who reproduces, distributes, or displays the work without the owner's permission.[34]

Under the 1976 act, authors were required to put a copyright notice on their works which included: (1) the symbol © or the words "copyright" or "copr.," (2) the year of publication, and (3) the name of the author. Since a 1989 change in the law, authors are no longer required to place a copyright notice on their works.[35] But it is wise to do so, since such a notice prohibits anyone from claiming that they innocently infringed a copyright. To be more fully protected, authors must register their work with the U.S. Copyright Office within three months after the work is published.[36] Copyright owners who do not register may still sue for damages. But by registering with the Copyright Office, copyright owners may be entitled to substantial "statutory damages" and attorney's fees.[37]

Works created after 1978 have copyrights that last until 50 years after the death of the author. Copyright owners can sell or transfer their ownership and give someone else the right to make and distribute copies. When two authors collaborate on a joint work, they both own a right to the entire work and each can transfer his or her interest without asking permission of the coauthor.

Do Teachers Own a Copyright on Works They Produce at School?

Not usually. Teachers may create lesson plans, books, and other teaching materials that they wish to copyright. Under a rule known as "work made for hire," however, the employer of the teacher is considered to be the author; the employee who actually created the work does not own the copyright. Thus, the copyright to any materials that teachers produce within the scope of their employment is owned by the school district.

On the other hand, teachers who act as "independent contractors" can obtain a copyright. A reading teacher, for example, might agree to produce materials for the school district. If the district relies on the teacher's expertise, specially compensates the teacher for this project, requests that the teacher use his or her own equipment and resources, and otherwise gives the teacher complete freedom in structuring the materials, the teacher could be considered an independent contractor and not subject to the work-for-hire doctrine. A teacher could also avoid the application of this doctrine by signing a contract with the employer limiting the employer's rights in two ways. First, the contract could specify that certain types of activities, such as any materials presented at national professional meetings, will not be considered within the scope of employment. Second, the contract could give the teacher rights other than ownership of the copyright. For example, under such terms, the employer, which still owns the copyright, could give the teacher the right to reproduce or distribute curriculum materials.

Does Copyright Law Apply to the Internet?

Yes. The basic doctrines of copyright law protect works appearing on and distributed via the Internet.

Fair Use: When Can Copyrighted Works Be Copied without Permission?

The doctrine of fair use is an exception to the general rules of copyright law that allows use of copyrighted material without the user's securing the copyright owner's consent. The doctrine is designed to balance the exclusive rights of the copyright owner against the public's interest in dissemination of information. When determining whether a particular use of copyrighted material is fair use, courts consider the purpose of the fair use doctrine and the following four statutory criteria:

1. the purpose and character of the use, including whether such use is of a commercial nature or is for a nonprofit educational purpose;
2. the nature of the copyrighted work;
3. the amount used in relation to the copyrighted work as a whole; and
4. the effect of the use on the potential market for the copyrighted work.[38]

Are There Fair Use Exceptions for Teachers?

Yes. Teachers are permitted to make *single* copies of the following copyrighted works for their own use in scholarly research or classroom preparation:[39] (1) a chapter from a book; (2) an article from a periodical or newspaper; (3) a short story, short essay, or short poem; and (4) a chart, graph, diagram, drawing, cartoon, or picture from a book, newspaper, or periodical.

In addition, a teacher can make multiple copies of the following copyrighted works for use in the classroom (with the number of copies not to exceed one copy per student in the class), provided that copying meets certain tests of brevity, spontaneity, and cumulative effect and that each copy includes a notice of copyright. The definition of *brevity* is:

- a complete poem or excerpt, if it is less than 250 words;
- a complete article, story, or essay if it is less than 2,500 words;

- an excerpt from a prose work, if it is less than 1,000 words or 10 percent of the work, whichever is less; or
- one chart, diagram, cartoon, or picture per book or periodical.

The definition of *spontaneity* means that:

- the copying is at the instance and inspiration of the individual teacher, and
- the inspiration and decision to use the work and the moment of its use for maximum teaching effectiveness are so close in time that it would be unreasonable to expect a timely reply to a request for permission.

To meet the test of *cumulative effect* the copying of the material:

- must be for only one course;
- must not involve more than one short poem, article, story, essay; or two excerpts from the same author, or more than three from the same collective work or periodical volume during one class term; and
- must not involve more than nine instances of such multiple copying for one course during one class term.[40]

However, teachers cannot make copies of "consumable" materials, such as workbooks or answer sheets to standardized tests.

In addition to the exceptions for copying, the act also exempts certain public performances. For example, the performance of a copyrighted dramatic work by students and teachers in the classroom is not a copyright violation. If students give a "public performance" of a copyrighted work, however, they will be protected from copyright violation only when there is no admission charge and no compensation paid to any performer or promoter. Even when students perform without pay, if the school charges admission to the performance, the copyright owner has the right to prohibit the performance. Teachers who do not follow these guidelines can be held liable for copyright infringement.

Is It Fair Use to Copy Computer Software for Educational Purposes?

Not usually. Computer programs are eligible for copyright protection, and therefore making copies of software for students is not fair use. However, the owner of a copyright program does not infringe the copyright by making one copy for backup purposes only.[41] Because it is so easy to copy computer software, schools should be careful to educate students and teachers about illegal copying.[42]

Is It Fair Use to Videotape for Educational Purposes?

Although federal law does not include specific rules for educational videotaping, a committee of copyright proprietors and educational organizations developed guidelines that apply to off-air recording by nonprofit educational institutions.[43] These guidelines provide that such institutions may videotape copyrighted television programs, but may keep the tape only for 45 days, after which it must be destroyed. During 10 school days after the taping, teachers may use the tape for instructional purposes and may repeat such use only once for instructional reinforcement. After the 10 days, the tape may only be used to evaluate its educational usefulness.

Where Can Teachers Get Permission to Photograph or Videotape Where There Is No Fair Use Exception?

In such cases, teachers should get written permission to copy or tape from the copyright owner. In requesting permission, the teacher should specify the exact material to be copied, the number of copies, and the proposed use of the materials.

What Are the Penalties for Violating a Copyright?

In a suit for copyright infringement, a court may issue an injunction to prevent people from making further copies and may order the destruction of all illegal copies. In addition, the copyright owner can collect lost profits or an amount ranging from $500 to $20,000 for an infringement of one work to as much as $100,000 for intentional violations or as little as $200 for unintentional violations.[44]

Guidelines

Criticizing School Policy or Personnel

- To determine whether a teacher's out-of-class speech is protected by the First Amendment, courts first determine whether the speech is about a personal grievance or a matter of public concern. If it is about a personal matter, it is not protected.
- If the speech is about issues of public concern, courts will use a "balancing test." They will balance the interest of a teacher as a citizen in commenting

on matters of public interest against the interest of the government in promoting the efficient operation of the schools.

- The balance will likely favor teachers who publicly criticize how schools raise funds, whose criticism relates to violations of students' rights or dangers to their health or safety, or to illegal practices.
- The balance will likely favor the school when teachers' public statements involve disclosures of confidential information, false or misleading accusations about superiors or colleagues, or complaints about classroom assignments or personal evaluations.

Academic Freedom

- School boards have broad discretion to determine the curriculum and to require or prohibit specific texts.
- Administrators may require approval of supplementary material. However, teachers should not be disciplined for using controversial materials or methods unless they know (or should know) that the materials or methods are prohibited.

Freedom of Association

- Teachers cannot be fired for mere membership in a subversive or controversial organization unless they support the organization's unlawful aims or activities.
- Teachers have a right to send their children to private or public schools.
- Teachers can be prohibited from marrying administrators.
- Teachers can be punished for having sexual relations with former students within one or two years of graduation if it is against school district policy.
- Laws differ about whether teachers can run for partisan political office. Teachers are usually prohibited from running for the school board where they teach to avoid conflicts of interest. But, most districts allow teachers to run for part-time, nonpartisan positions that do not interfere with their teaching.

Dress and Grooming

- Schools have broad discretion to regulate teachers' dress and grooming.
- Teachers cannot be punished for violating such regulations without adequate due process.

Copyright

- The federal Copyright Act protects not only creative written work but other pictorial or graphic expressions on videotape or computer disk.

- To establish a copyright, authors place a copyright notice on all copies of their work. Additional protections are available to copyright owners who register their work with the federal Copyright Office.

- When teachers create material within the scope of their employment, the copyright is owned by the school district. However, teachers who work as independent contractors can obtain their own copyright.

- Fair use is an exception to copyright law that allows teachers to use a limited amount of copyrighted materials for educational purposes without the owner's consent.

Notes

1. *Pickering v. Bd. of Educ.*, 391 U.S. 563 (1968).
2. *Lusk v. Estes*, 361 F. Supp. 653 (N.D. Tex. 1973).
3. *Anderson v. Evans*, 660 F.2d 153 (6th Cir. 1981).
4. *Connick v. Myers*, 462 U.S. 138 (1983).
5. *Hesse v. Bd. of Educ. of Township High Sch. Dist. No. 211*, 848 F.2d 748 (7th Cir. 1988).
6. *Ifill v. Dist. of Columbia*, 665 A.2d 185 (D.C. 1995).
7. *Connick v. Myers*, 462 U.S. 138 (1983)
8. *Lifton v. Bd. of Educ. of Chicago*, 290 F. Supp. 2d 940 (N.D. Ill. 2003).
9. *Cirelli v. Johnston Sch. Dist.*, 897 F. Supp. 663 (D. R.I. 1995).
10. *Chicago Sch. Reform Bd. of Tr. v. Substance, Inc.*, 79 F. Supp. 2d 919 (N.D. Ill. 2000).
11. *Keefe v. Geanakos*, 418 F.2d 359 (1st Cir. 1969).
12. *Virgil v. Sch. Bd. of Columbia Cnty., Fla.*, 862 F.2d 1517 (11th Cir. 1989).
13. *Bd. of Ed., Island Trees Union Free Sch. Dist. No. 26 v. Pico*, 457 U.S. 853 (1982).
14. *Sterzing v. Fort Bend Indep. Sch. Dist.*, 376 F. Supp. 657 (S.D. Tex. 1972).
15. *Kirkland v. Northside Indep. Sch. Dist.*, 890 F.2d 794 (5th Cir. 1989).
16. *Peloza v. Capistrano Unified Sch. Dist.*, 782 F. Supp. 1412 (C.D. Cal. 1992).
17. *Brubaker v. Bd. of Educ. Sch. Dist. No. 149, Cook Cnty., Ill*, 502 F.2d 973 (7th Cir. 1974).
18. *Fowler v. Bd. of Educ.*, 819 F.2d 657 (6th Cir. 1987).
19. *Reitmeyer v. Unemployment Cmpensation Bd. of Review*, 602 A.2d 505 (Pa. Commw. 1992).
20. *Mailloux v. Kiley*, 323 F. Supp. 1387 (D. Mass. 1971).
21. *Ward v. Hickey*, 996 F.2d 448 (1st Cir. 1993).

22. *Bernstein v. Norwich City Sch. Dist.,* 726 N.Y.S.2d 474 (A.D. 3 Dept. 2001).
23. *Hetrick v. Martin,* 480 F.2d 705 (6th Cir. 1973).
24. *Mailloux* at 1392.
25. *Healy v. James,* 408 U.S. 169 (1972).
26. *Melzer v. Bd. of Educ. of the City of New York,* 336 F.3d 185 (2nd Cir. 2003).
27. *Barrett v. Steubenville City Sch.,* 388 F.3d 967 (6th Cir. 2004).
28. *Keckeisen v. Indep. Sch. Dist. No. 612,* 509 F.2d 1062 (8th Cir. 1975).
29. *Solomon v. Quinones,* 531 N.Y.S.2d 349 (N.Y. App. Div. 1988).
30. *Flashkamp v. Dearborn Public Schools,* 385 F.3d 935 (6th Cir. 2004).
31. *Miller v. Sch. Dist. No. 167,* 495 F.2d 658 (7th Cir. 1974).
32. *Blanchet v. Vermilion Parish Sch. Bd.,* 220 So.2d 534 (La. 1969).
33. *Lucia v. Duggan,* 303 F. Supp. 112 (D. Mass. 1969).
34. Copyright Act of 1876, 17 U.S. C. §§ 101-1010.
35. 17 U.S.C. § 401 (d).
36. For information on how to register, see the U.S. Copyright Office Website at www. loc.gov/copyright.
37. Kenneth Crews, *Copyright Law for Librarians & Educators* (2nd ed., American Library Association 2006), p. 80.
38. 17 U.S.C. § 107.
39. Notes of Committee on the Judiciary, H.R. No. 94-1476, 94th Cong. (1976).
40. Numbers 2 and 3 of the cumulative effect test do not apply to current news periodicals and newspapers.
41. 17 U.S.C. § 117.
42. For a model school district software policy, see John Soma & Dwight Pringle, *"Computer Software in the Public Schools,"* 28 *Education Law Reporter,* 315, 323–24 (1985).
43. Guidelines for Off-Air Recording of Broadcast Programming for Educational Purposes, 97 *Cong. Rec.* E4751 daily ed. (Oct. 14, 1981).
44. 17 U.S.C. § 501(b).

Student Freedom of Expression

Speech, Press, Association, and Appearance

When conflicts arise between the rights of students and educators about freedom of expression, judges balance the rights in conflict and determine when to protect and when to limit this freedom. In resolving these conflicts, courts establish legal principles and precedents that apply to future cases. On the basis of these principles, this chapter explains when student freedoms of speech and of the press are protected, the laws applying to student organizations, and when schools can regulate students' personal appearance.

Free Speech Issues

Does Freedom of Speech Apply to Students in Public Schools?

Yes. In the landmark case of *Tinker v. Des Moines,* the U.S. Supreme Court ruled that students do not "shed their Constitutional right to freedom of speech or expression at the schoolhouse gate."[1] The case concerned students who were suspended for wearing black armbands to protest against the war in Vietnam. According to the Court, "Students in school as well as out of school are . . . possessed of fundamental rights which the State must respect, just as they themselves must respect their obligations to the State." Since schools are "educating the young for citizenship," they should protect the "Constitutional freedoms of the individual, if we are not to strangle the free mind at its source and teach youth to discount important principles of our government as mere platitudes." Thus, in *Tinker,* the Court ruled that students had the constitutional right to wear black armbands as a protected form of symbolic speech.

The Court realized that protecting controversial speech might be a risk. In fact, it recognized that "any word spoken, in class, in the lunchroom, or on the campus, that deviates from the views of another person may start an argument or cause a disturbance." According to the Court, however, "our Constitution says we must take this risk; and our history says that it is this sort of hazardous freedom— this kind of openness—that is the basis of our national strength . . . independence and vigor."[2]

Does *Tinker* Apply to Elementary Schools?

The answer is uncertain since judges are not in agreement about this question. Recent court cases suggest that even where the *Tinker* ruling has been applied, first- or third-graders may not have the same free expression rights as secondary students. As one judge wrote: "a school's authority to control speech in an elementary school setting is undoubtedly greater than in a high school."[3]

Is Disruptive Speech Protected?

No. Despite the breadth of the *Tinker* decision, it also recognized that schools can legally limit student expression. In *Tinker,* the Court identified that limit when it wrote that any student conduct which "materially disrupts classwork or involves substantial disorder or invasion of the rights of others" is not protected. Thus, a federal appeals court allowed administrators to enforce a "no-button" rule in a Cleveland high school because evidence indicated that such symbols led to serious fighting between black and white students and substantially disrupted the education process.[4] Furthermore, schools do not have to wait until a disruption takes place to limit speech. Thus, a judge explained that a school official may restrict student expression when there is significant evidence of a "reasonable likelihood of substantial disorder."[5]

Is Obscene Speech Protected?

No. To be legally obscene, material must violate three tests developed by the Supreme Court: (1) it must appeal to the prurient or lustful interest; (2) it must describe sexual conduct in a way that is "patently offensive" to community standards; *and* (3) taken as a whole, it "must lack serious literary, artistic, political, or scientific value."[6]

Can School Administrators Prohibit and Punish Vulgar and Offensive Speech That Is Not Legally Obscene or Disruptive?

Yes, ruled the Supreme Court in a case involving Matthew Fraser, who was punished for giving a nominating speech at a high school assembly that referred to his candidate using "an elaborate, graphic, and explicit sexual metaphor."[7] In *Bethel v. Fraser,* the Court ruled that school officials have broad authority to punish students for using "offensively lewd and indecent speech" in classrooms, assemblies, and other school-sponsored educational activities—even if the speech does not cause disruption and is not legally obscene. In addition, *Bethel* held that administrators have discretion to define and determine what constitutes vulgar and offensive speech. Whether students can display the controversial sign "Bong Hits 4 Jesus" is now before the Supreme Court.

Are School-Sponsored, Curricular Publications Protected?

No. The First Amendment does not protect student freedom of the press in school-sponsored, curricular publications. Thus, the U.S. Supreme Court, in *Hazelwood v. Kuhlmeier,* ruled in favor of a high school principal who censored two stories about pregnancy and divorce in a student newspaper that were written as part of a journalism course.[8] The Court explained that when a student expresses personal, controversial views on school grounds, such views are protected by the First Amendment and the principles of *Tinker* apply. However, in school-sponsored publications or theatrical productions, educators may exercise substantial control. In a curricular publication, wrote the Court, educators may prohibit articles that are "ungrammatical, poorly written, inadequately researched, biased or prejudiced, vulgar or profane, or unsuitable for immature audiences."

Hazelwood, however, does not permit educators to censor school-sponsored publications unless they have a valid educational purpose. Similarly, the Supreme Court has ruled that school boards do not have unlimited discretion to censor library books, to deny student access to ideas for narrowly partisan or political reasons or simply because the board dislikes the ideas contained in those books.[9] More recently, a federal court ruled against an Arkansas school district that restricted access to Harry Potter books because of unfounded fears that they might promote disruption, witchcraft, and disobedience to parents.[10]

Although no public school in any state can provide less protection for student speech than is required by the U.S. Supreme Court, individual states or school districts can provide more. Thus, in the aftermath of *Hazelwood,* a few states—through statute or judicial interpretation—now have greater protection for student expression. For example, the California Education Code states: "Students of the public schools shall have the right to exercise freedom of speech and of the press . . . whether or not such publications . . . are supported financially by the school. . . ."[11]

Are Students' Underground Publications Protected?

Yes. The Supreme Court decision in *Hazelwood* does not give school officials control over the style and content of underground student periodicals, which are published without school sponsorship and are not part of the curriculum. Instead, *Tinker* governs such publications and their distribution usually cannot be prohibited unless schools have evidence to forecast that they will cause substantial disruption, interfere with the rights of others, or promote illegal activities. Therefore, underground publications cannot be banned for discussing unpopular or controversial topics, and students cannot be punished merely for criticizing school officials or administrative policies in these publications. However, schools are permitted to enforce content-neutral policies that regulate the time, place, and manner for distributing publications.

Students may be required to submit their publications to administrators for review before distribution. The justification for allowing prior review of underground publications, explained one judge, is "to prevent disruption and not to stifle expression."[12]

Are Message T-Shirts Protected?

Generally, they are, and judges usually apply the principles of *Tinker* in these cases. This was illustrated by a 2003 controversy in Michigan, when a high school student wore a T-shirt with a picture of President Bush above the caption "International Terrorist." Administrators banned the shirt because it was "inappropriate" and might be disruptive. Since there was no evidence that the T-shirt caused or was likely to cause substantial disruption, a federal court ruled that the ban violated the student's First Amendment rights.[13] However, schools can prohibit T-shirts that promote drugs, alcohol, or illegal behavior.

Can Schools Restrict Cell Phones?

Yes. Concerns about inappropriate student use of cell phones have led 10 states to prohibit such phones in school, and 17 states have granted local districts authority to prohibit them.[14] Even without legislation, schools have authority to prohibit cell phone use that causes disruption, cheating, or interferes with the rights of others (such as taking secret photographs).

On the other hand, an increasing number of students in grades 3–12 use cell phones in or after school. Many parents, in cities such as New York, want their children to carry cell phones to and from school for safety reasons. And in some states, such as New Hampshire, schools encourage students to use Web-based cell phones to access homework and class assignments. Thus, policies concerning cell phone use vary among our states and school districts.

Can Schools Restrict the Use of School Computers?

Yes. Schools have broad discretion to develop policies that allow school computers to be used only for specific educational purposes. Policies can prohibit such inappropriate uses as violations of copyright laws, harassment of students or staff, commercial purposes, and search or transmission of pornographic material. Furthermore, students can be required to sign an agreement stating that they understand the policy before receiving a password and computer account.

In addition, the Children's Internet Protection Act requires public schools to use filters that protect against access to obscene material and to child pornography. Schools can install software to filter the World Wide Web by blocking sites known to harbor explicit sexual material, or they can subscribe to online services that offer similar control options. If students challenge policies that restrict Internet use in school, judges probably will uphold the restrictions if they have an educational purpose and are not arbitrary.

Can Schools Punish Students for Offensive Messages on Their Home Computers?

In contrast to educators' broad discretion to restrict the use of school computers, administrators have limited authority to restrict and punish students' offensive use of their home computers. In a Missouri case, for example, a high school student was suspended for creating a Web page at home that used vulgar language and was critical of teachers and administrators. Applying the *Tinker* test, the court ruled in favor of the student since the Web page caused no disruption.[15] On the other hand, a Pennsylvania court upheld the expulsion of a middle school student who posted a Website at home that harassed and threatened his algebra teacher and had a profoundly disruptive effect.[16] In sum, students should not be punished for posting an offensive, insulting, or vulgar home page on the Internet unless it causes substantial disruption at school.

Do Student Blogs Pose Special Problems?

Yes. Blogs are Websites where entries may be posted on a regular basis and frequently serve as online commentaries. While student bloggers are responsible for the messages they create, they cannot be held responsible for content added by third parties. Thus, when a New Jersey student blogger was suspended after another student added extremely offensive material to his blog, a federal court ruled that the school violated the blogger's First Amendment rights because he was not responsible for the postings of other students.[17]

Is a Threat Protected Speech?

Not if it is a "true threat." Such a threat is unprotected if a reasonable person would interpret the statement as "a serious expression of an intent to do harm." In a Michigan case, however, a student successfully challenged his expulsion for creating "Satan's web page" at home "for laughs" that included a mock list of people he wished would die. The judge ruled that this was not a true threat since no reasonable person would think the Website expressed a serious intent to harm anyone and therefore was protected speech.[18]

Is Criticism of Teachers Protected?

Not if it is disrespectful, insubordinate, or disruptive. Thus, a student's letter to her basketball teammates that was highly critical of her coach and said "it is time to give him back some of the bullshit he has given us," was considered "insubordinate speech" and not protected by the First Amendment.[19]

Association

Is Freedom of Association a Right of Public School Students?

While courts have broadly protected freedom of association among adults, its application to students in public schools has been much narrower. For example, a federal court upheld a Minnesota high school rule that permitted student athletes to be punished for "attending parties where alcohol and/or illegal drugs . . . are present."[20] The court ruled that the student's "desire to associate socially with his peers at parties" is not a form of association entitled to constitutional protection. Similarly, courts have upheld school rules prohibiting students from joining undemocratic fraternities, sororities, or secret clubs.

Does the Equal Access Act Protect Controversial Student Organizations?

Partly. The federal Equal Access Act prohibits any public secondary school from discriminating against any student group on the basis of the "religious, political, philosophical, or other content" of its views if the school permits any noncurricular group to meet during noninstructional time.[21] Therefore, schools must permit student religious clubs and gay/straight alliances to meet on the same basis as any other extracurricular organization.

Does Recognition of an Organization Imply Approval of Its Goals?

No. The purpose of recognition is to enable schools to be informed about the purposes and activities of an organization and to ensure that students are willing to comply with school rules that govern the time, place, and manner in which groups may function. There might be less misunderstanding if schools "registered" rather than recognized student organizations.

When Can Schools Deny Access to a Student Group?

When the school prohibits all student clubs or when the club is noncurricular and the school only permits curriculum-related groups. Furthermore, the Equal Access Act allows schools to restrict student groups "to maintain order" and "to protect the well-being of students."

Personal Appearance

Do Students Have a Right to Wear Their Hair as They Wish?

Courts are deeply divided over this issue. About half the federal appeals courts say they have such a right. These are some of the arguments courts have used to uphold grooming as a constitutional freedom:

- It is a personal liberty protected by the Fourteenth Amendment since "compelled conformity to conventional standards" is not a justifiable part of education.[22]
- Long hair is a form of symbolic speech by which students convey their individuality, and it is protected by the First Amendment.
- Prohibiting boys but not girls from wearing long hair is a denial of equal protection.

In contrast, about half the courts uphold policies that restrict student grooming. These judges say grooming is not a constitutional right because hair length is usually a matter of personal taste, not a specific message; because grooming regulations do not restrict a fundamental constitutional liberty; and because courts cannot protect citizens against every minor restriction on their freedom.

Why Has the U.S. Supreme Court Not Resolved the Grooming Conflict?

Usually, when federal appeals courts differ in their interpretation of the Constitution, the Supreme Court resolves the conflict and establishes a "uniform law of the land." But, the Supreme Court has declined to review these conflicting opinions because most of the justices do not believe the issue is of national significance.

Can I Know How Federal Courts Might Rule on Grooming Cases in My State?

Yes. Since the Supreme Court has refused to hear these cases, the law will be governed by the decisions of the federal circuit courts, and they have all indicated directly or indirectly how they would probably rule. Thus, Figure 5.1 indicates whether grooming is a constitutional right in your state.

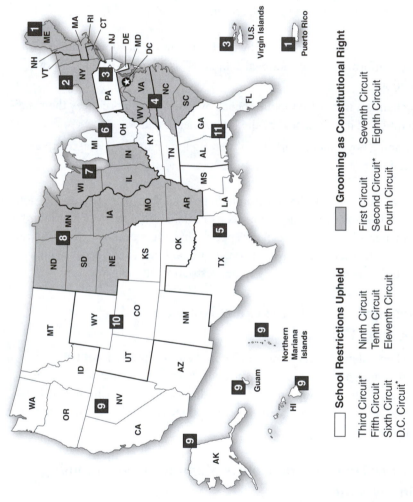

Figure 5.1 ● Circuit Court Rulings on Grooming

Source: 28 USCA, Section 41.

Can Grooming Laws Be Challenged under State Law?

Yes. Students and parents who live in circuits which have held that grooming is not a constitutional right can still challenge grooming policies under state law. Some state judges believe that grooming rules which only apply to boys violate their state's equal rights amendment (ERA) or antidiscrimination laws. In contrast, other judges have refused to use their ERA to "micro-manage" high schools and have ruled that dress and grooming codes that "differentiate" between males and females is not discrimination "because of sex." Thus, there are sharp differences among state judges just as there are among the federal courts.

Can Schools Regulate Student Clothing?

Yes. All courts agree that schools have authority to regulate student clothing if they have an educational rationale. In 2005, for example, a federal court in Kentucky upheld a detailed middle school dress code because it does not restrict a particular viewpoint, and it advances important educational interests, including focusing attention on learning, increasing school unity and pride, reducing discipline problems, improving self-respect, decreasing distractions, producing cost savings, and bridging economic gaps between families.[23]

Can Schools Require School Uniforms?

Yes, and such requirements have been upheld for the reasons noted above. When some parents argued that uniforms would create a financial burden, one court pointed out that uniforms cost no more than normal clothing and are donated to those who cannot afford them.

Is Wearing Ethnic Clothing a Protected Form of Expression?

It might be if it meets a two-part test: (1) if it conveys a "particular message" and (2) if it is likely that the message would be understood by an observer. However, this test did not protect a New Mexico student who wore "sagging pants" to express his "links with black culture" in violation of school rules. A judge ruled that the student failed to show that wearing the pants conveyed "an objectively recognizable message" that an observer would understand.[24]

Does a "No Hats" Policy Violate Students' Rights?

Not usually. In a Maryland case, a judge noted with approval some of a school's reasons for the policy: wearing hats could increase horseplay, block teachers' view of students and students' view of teachers, allow students to hide drugs and cheat sheets, and foster a less respectful learning climate.[25] However, it is likely that a student's nondisruptive religious head covering would be protected.

Can Schools Ban Earrings, Jewelry, and Other Symbols of Gang Membership?

Yes. Even courts that have held rules against long hair to be unconstitutional will uphold bans against gang symbols if they directly relate to student safety. Even if the ban on jewelry only applies to men, it will probably be upheld where men, not women, wear jewelry to indicate gang membership.

However, such bans may be challenged where there is no evidence of gang activity. Furthermore, broad prohibitions of "gang-related activities" may be void for vagueness when they fail to provide adequate notice to students about what conduct is prohibited or when they allow for arbitrary or subjective enforcement.

Can Schools Ban Confederate Flag Symbols?

They can where the flag has been associated with racial hostility, disruption, or violence.

Guidelines

- The First Amendment applies to students in public schools. This means that students cannot be punished for expressing controversial political, religious, or educational views unless they cause substantial disruption or interfere with the rights of others. This freedom of expression applies to student speech, writing, and usually to message T-shirts.

- Educators have broad discretion to regulate student expression in school-sponsored activities such as curricular publications and school plays. Thus, teachers can define and punish lewd and vulgar language in classrooms, assemblies, and other educational programs.

- In most states, educators can control student publications that are not part of the curriculum if they are school-sponsored, teacher-supervised educational activities. Since some states provide greater protection for extracurricular publications, teachers should check state and district policies before restricting such publications.

- Educators have broad control over the use of computers in school, but they should not punish students for posting offensive messages on their home computers unless they substantially disrupt school activities.

- Educators cannot prohibit students from distributing publications because they advocate a particular religious, political, or social view. However, schools can establish viewpoint-neutral policies that regulate the time, place, and manner for distributing materials.

- The Equal Access Act prohibits secondary schools from discriminating against any student organization because of its views.

- Courts are divided about whether schools can prohibit boys from wearing long hair. However, all schools may regulate student clothing, prohibit hats, and require uniforms if they wish. In addition, schools may ban jewelry and other symbols of gang membership.

Notes

1. *Tinker v. Des Moines*, 393 U.S. 503 (1969).
2. *Id.* at 508–509.
3. *S.G. ex rel. A.G. v. Sayerville Bd. of Educ.*, 333 F.3d 417 (3rd Cir. 2003).
4. *Guzick v. Drebus*, 431 F.2d 594 (6th Cir. 1970), *cert. denied*, 401 U.S. 948 (1971).
5. *Karp v. Becken*, 477 F.2d 171 (9th Cir. 1973).
6. *Miller v. California*, 413 U.S. 15 (1973).
7. *Bethel Sch. Dist. No. 403 v. Fraser*, 478 U.S. 675 (1986).
8. *Hazelwood Sch. Dist. v. Kuhlmeier*, 484 U.S. 260 (1988).
9. *Bd. of Educ., Island Trees Union Free Sch. Dist. No. 26 v. Pico*, 457 U.S. 853 (1982).
10. *Counts v. Cedarville Sch. Dist.*, 295 F. Supp. 2d 996 (W.D. Ark. 2003).
11. California Education Code, § 48907 (1991).
12. *Shanley v. Northeast Indep. Sch. Dist.*, 462 F.2d 960 (5th Cir. 1972).
13. *Barber v. Dearborn Public Schools*, 286 F. Supp. 2d 847 (E.D. Mich. 2003).
14. A. Dean Pickett & Christopher Thomas, "21st Century Intrusion Into Learning," *A Legal Memorandum* (National Association of Secondary School Principals, Summer, 2005).
15. *Beussink v. Woodland R-IV Sch. Dist.*, 30 F. Supp. 2d 1175 (E.D. Mo. 1998).
16. *J. S. v. Bethlehem Area Sch. Dist.*, 757 A.2d 412 (Pa. Commw. Ct. 2000).
17. Elizabeth Kirby & Brenda Kallio, "Blogs: A New Frontier for School Discipline," *A Legal Memorandum* (National Association of Secondary School Principals, Fall, 2006), p. 3.
18. *Mahaffey v. Aldrich*, 236 F. Supp. 2d 779 (E.D. Mich. 2002).
19. *Wildman v. Marshalltown Sch. Dist.*, 249 F.3d 768 (8th Cir. 2001).
20. *Bush v. Dassel-Cakato Bd. of Educ.*, 745 F. Supp. 562 (D. Minn. 1990).
21. 20 U.S.C.A. § 4071 (a) and (b) (2000).
22. *Richards v. Thurston*, 424 F.2d 1281 (1st Cir. 1970).
23. *Blau v. Ft. Thomas Public Sch. Dist.*, 401 F.3d 381 (6th Cir. 2005).
24. *Bevins v. Albuquerque Pub. Sch.*, 899 F. Supp. 556 (D. N.M. 1995).
25. *Isaacs v. Bd. of Educ. of Howard County*, 40 F. Supp. 2d 335 (D. Md. 1999).

chapter 6

Due Process Rights of Teachers and Students

The U.S. Constitution establishes the right to due process of law in both the Fifth and Fourteenth Amendments. We focus on the latter, for public schools are agencies of the state and the Fourteenth Amendment provides that no "State shall deprive any person of life, liberty, or property, without due process of law." Because the actions of teachers, administrators, and school board members are state actions, the Fourteenth Amendment applies to them. It also applies to students, because courts have held that the right to attend public schools is a *property* right protected by the same amendment.

Due Process

In ordinary language, due process means fair procedures, and it requires that official action not be arbitrary, unreasonable, or discriminatory. The meaning of these terms becomes clear through court decisions.

Do All Teachers Have the Same Right to Due Process?

No. There is a significant difference in the due process rights of tenured and non-tenured teachers as discussed in Chapter 2. Because tenured teachers have a right to continuous employment, this grants them a *property* right, which the Fourteenth Amendment protects. Probationary teachers have a right to their job only during the term of their contract, usually one year. If they are not reappointed, they are not deprived of any property. They do have a right to a hearing if constitutionally impermissible grounds were the reasons for not being reappointed, for example, if they were not reappointed for unionizing activities, for exercising their free speech rights, or for membership in a controversial organization. They also have a right to a hearing if the reasons given for not being reappointed were *stigmatizing* and thus damaging their opportunities for future employment. This would damage their *liberty* interest or professional reputation protected by the Fourteenth Amendment. An accusation of racism or gender discrimination in the classroom would be stigmatizing and would merit a hearing to challenge the accusation.

Teachers with tenure have full due process rights, that is, a right to fair proceedings *prior* to any administrative decision that would have a negative impact on their employment. Chapter 2 describes the protections afforded tenured teachers in due process hearings.

Do Students Have a Right to Due Process?

Every state provides public education between certain ages and students have a *property* right to such education, protected by the Fourteenth Amendment. They cannot be deprived of that right without due process.

Can Students Be Suspended without Due Process?

No. Dwight Lopez was a high school student in Columbus, Ohio, when some demonstrations occurred and disturbances broke out in school. He and several other students were suspended for up to 10 days without a hearing. Dwight claimed that he was an innocent bystander and that he was never informed of what he was accused of doing. Dwight and other suspended students sued in a federal court, claiming a denial of their due process rights, and a trial court agreed with them. When the administrators appealed, the Supreme Court, in a 5–4 decision, ruled in favor of the students.[1]

Do students retain their constitutional rights when they enter a school? Citing the *Tinker* case, the Supreme Court said yes. Writing for the majority, Justice White stated that, while states are not required to establish schools, once they do, students acquire a property right in them, which may not be withdrawn without "fundamentally fair procedures." Clearly, said the Court, the Constitution protects students in cases of expulsion from the public schools.

But is there a similar protection in cases of short-term suspension? Yes. A suspension of up to 10 days is not so minor a punishment that it may be imposed "in complete disregard of the Due Process Clause," wrote Justice White. Such exclusion is a serious event in the life of a child, and it becomes even more serious if the misconduct is recorded in the student's file. A record of the suspension is likely to damage the student's standing with teachers and hurt his or her opportunities for higher education and employment.

Is the Due Process Requirement Always the Same for All Types of Suspensions?

No. While the Court indicated that some due process is required for short-term suspensions of one to ten days, this can be quite informal. Students should be given oral or written notification of the charges against them and the possible punishment. They should have an opportunity to admit or refute the accusation before an objective decision maker. They should also be told what evidence there is against them and be given an opportunity to tell their side of the story.

All this can be done quite informally and may follow immediately the alleged rule infraction. In subsequent cases, the Court made it clear that in conflicts which might call for short suspension, the student does not have a right to counsel or to cross-examine witnesses. A possible short suspension does not trigger the full range of procedural protection applicable to criminal prosecutions.[2] Furthermore, the *Miranda warning* is also inapplicable to school disciplinary situations since it basically applies to criminal cases where the courts apply the due process clause of the Fifth Amendment.

Some states by statute go beyond the requirements specified in *Goss*. For example, both Pennsylvania and Ohio require written notice of the intent to suspend and the reasons for it prior to the informal hearing.

What Rights Do Students Have Prior to Long-Term Suspension or Expulsion?

Because long-term suspensions or expulsion constitute greater deprivation of property rights, the courts require more thorough, meticulous procedures to protect students' rights. State laws and school board policies generally specify procedural requirements that must be followed prior to long-term suspension or expulsion. These usually include:

- written notice of the charges and intention to expel or suspend;
- time and place of the hearing with ample time to prepare;
- a full and fair hearing before an impartial tribunal;
- a right to legal counsel or representation by parents or other adults;
- a right to know the evidence used against the student;
- an opportunity to present witnesses and evidence and to cross-examine witnesses;
- a written record of the decision and the evidence on which it was based; and
- a right to appeal.

It is clear from this list that significant differences exist in the due process requirements applicable to short-term and long-term suspensions and expulsion. As indicated in Chapter 8, special requirements apply to disciplinary situations involving disabled students.

What about Students Who Bring Guns, Other Dangerous Weapons, or Drugs to School?

The No Child Left Behind Act of 2003, along with other state laws and board policies, provides for so-called *zero-tolerance policies* with severe disciplinary consequences, including at least a 1-year expulsion for bringing weapons or drugs to school. These policies have received much criticism for their inflexibility, and courts have interpreted them differently.

Is Due Process Required before Every Minor Punishment?

No. There are countless numbers of minor disciplinary infractions in schools, such as whispering at quiet times, chewing gum, not doing required work, and so on. When students receive minor punishments such as detention for these, no due process is required by law. By contrast, if students are violent or present a threat to themselves or others, they can be immediately removed from the situation and suspended with due process to follow as soon as practicable.

May Schools Use Corporal Punishment?

That depends on state law and board policy. Today at least 27 states prohibit corporal punishment either by law or administrative regulations. Many school boards forbid its use by district policy even in states that do not prohibit it by statute. And even in places that allow it, corporal punishment must be reasonable. A teacher who administers unreasonable corporal punishment may face charges of assault and battery as well as a civil suit for money damages. He or she may also be suspended or otherwise disciplined by the school district.

What kind of corporal punishment is reasonable? In the final analysis, the court decides this question by considering the student's age, size and weight, and maturity and past behavior; the instrument used, if any; the nature of the offense; harm to the student; and the motivation of the person administering the punishment.

Must Due Process Precede Corporal Punishment?

No, according to the courts, because that would dilute any effectiveness it might have due to the time delay between the infraction and punishment.

Is Excessive Corporal Punishment a Violation of the Constitution?

No, ruled the Supreme Court in *Ingraham v. Wright*.[3] The Court held that even excessive corporal punishment in schools does not violate the Eighth Amendment's prohibition of cruel and unusual punishment, which was intended to protect against the misuse of force in closed institutions such as prisons and not in schools that are relatively open to public scrutiny.

Excessive corporal punishment, however, probably violates other laws and policies. In addition, some federal appeals courts have held that such punishment may be so brutal as to violate a student's substantive due process rights, which protects individuals against arbitrary and unreasonable governmental action that is literally "shocking to the conscience."[4]

Teachers should be well acquainted with the laws and regulations in their particular state related to corporal punishment, as well as the policies of their local school board. Violation of the latter may be considered insubordination and may incur administrative punishment such as suspension and even dismissal.

Search and Seizure

Does the Constitution Apply to Searching Students?

Yes, it does, according to the Supreme Court's 1985 ruling in *New Jersey v. T.L.O.*[5] This case arose in a high school in New Jersey that had a rule forbidding smoking by students on school grounds. When a teacher walked into a girls' lavatory, she smelled smoke and saw T.L.O. and another student holding lighted cigarettes. The girls were escorted to the assistant principal's office. There, upon request, T.L.O. opened her purse where, in addition to cigarettes, there was drug paraphernalia and evidence that she had sold drugs. The vice principal called T.L.O.'s mother and the police.

The case eventually reached the Supreme Court, which held that the Fourth Amendment applies to searches of students by school officials. The majority of the Court rejected the Fourth Amendment requirement of probable cause or a search warrant as applicable to a school student. Instead, it used the standard of "reasonableness, under all the circumstances." The Court, in a two-step process, asked first whether the *initial* search was reasonable and, second, whether the *scope* of the search was reasonable under the circumstances. Justice White wrote that the initial search was reasonable in inception since finding cigarettes in the purse "would both corroborate the report that she had been smoking and undermine the credibility of her defense to the charge of smoking." Because the drug paraphernalia was plainly visible in the purse, the second search for marijuana was also considered reasonable in scope.

Whether a search is reasonable cannot be based on a subjective determination. The search of a student must be based on some objective facts or information received from reliable informants. The level of danger involved in the situation is also a significant factor in determining the reasonableness of the school's action. The Court in *T.L.O.* did not discuss the requirement of individualized suspicion, but courts in general protect an individual's expectation of privacy and don't leave it to the discretion of officials unless there is an exigency requiring immediate search.

May School Officials Search Students' Lockers?

Yes, they may, if they have a reasonable suspicion that the lockers contain something illegal or dangerous. Courts tend to hold that, since lockers are school property, and they are under the joint control of the schools and the student, the student has a lower expectation of privacy in them. This is particularly the case where school officials have a list of locker combinations and have periodically inspected them.

Some state laws or board policies specify guidelines for locker searches, which are usually published in student codes of conduct. A few states, such as Michigan for example, have declared by statute that a student who uses a school locker has no expectation of privacy in that locker or its contents. While in other states, for example in Pennsylvania, courts have followed *T.L.O.*, recognizing students' rights to privacy in their lockers and requiring reasonable suspicion on the part of school officials that lockers contain illegal or dangerous materials before they may be searched. Therefore, it is important for teachers or other school officials to know the law applicable in their particular state.

What If Police Are Involved in the Search of Students and Lockers?

There is no uniform law on police involvement in school searches. If school security officers are employed by a school district, their search activities are usually controlled by the *T.L.O.* standard of reasonable suspicion. On the other hand, if the police are involved in search for evidence related to a crime, they must have a warrant based on probable cause. In recent years, the courts tended to require the *probable cause* standard where police officers were involved in school searches rather than the less rigorous *reasonable suspicion* standard.

Can Students' Cars, Book Bags, Purses, and Other Property Be Searched?

Yes, they can be, under the reasonable suspicion standard of *T.L.O.* This standard does not require that school officials be absolutely certain before they search. As the Supreme Court noted, "sufficient probability, not certainty, is the touchstone of reasonableness under the Fourth Amendment."

Are School Officials Allowed to Strip Search Students?

Students have a high expectation of privacy in their person as well as the clothing they wear. "The Fourth Amendment applies with its fullest vigor against any intrusion on the human body."[6] While the *T.L.O.* standard applies to the search of pockets or purses, a strip search requires a more rigorous standard, akin to probable cause.

Since all relevant factors are considered by the courts to determine the constitutionality of a search, the courts are more likely to uphold the search if there are guns, other dangerous weapons, or drugs involved. Such a search must be based on individualized suspicion, carried out by an adult of the same gender as the student, and witnessed by another adult.

Courts differ in their conclusions regarding strip searches and are less likely to uphold them when the search involves money that disappeared. If the safety of students or danger to the school are involved, an individualized intrusive search is more likely to be upheld. The Sixth Circuit upheld the strip search of a high school female student where there was ample evidence that she was hiding drugs.[7] The search of a male high school student was also upheld when a large bulge in his sweatpants suggested to the school administrator that he was "crotching drugs."[8]

Can Schools Use Metal Detectors to Search for Weapons?

Yes, they can, particularly in high crime areas where guns and knives have often been brought to school. The use of metal detectors is not highly intrusive on one's privacy, while guns and knives in school represent a serious danger. Experience shows that the use of detectors significantly decreases the number of weapons brought to school.

Can Drug-Detecting Dogs Be Used in Schools?

With the widespread use of drugs in high schools, many communities began using trained dogs to detect the presence of drugs in lockers, cars, or in students' pockets and purses. Does the use of such dogs constitute a search? Courts have reached different conclusions on this question. Some concluded yes, while others held that the dogs' detecting the smell of drugs is analogous to the "plain view" doctrine and label it a "public smell" and therefore not a search.

As a general rule, courts have upheld the use of dogs to sniff objects such as lockers, cars, or desks. The dogs' behavior is insufficient evidence to justify a strip search. The Supreme Court has never ruled on this question and, until it does, disagreements among lower courts are likely to persist.

Can Schools Test Students for Drug Use?

Urinalysis is the most frequently used means of drug testing. It has been held constitutional by the Supreme Court as applied to students participating in interscholastic athletics. In *Vernonia v. Acton*,[9] there was widespread drug use among the athletes with a significant rise in disciplinary problems. Justice Scalia noted that "with regard to medical examinations and procedures . . . 'students within the school environment have a lesser expectation of privacy than members of the population generally.'" Furthermore, privacy expectations are even less for student athletes. As one example, he cited that in locker rooms "an element of 'communal undress' is inherent in athletic participation."

Furthermore, in 2002, the Supreme Court, in *Board of Education v. Earls,*[10] upheld a policy that called for suspicionless, random drug testing of students in all extracurricular activities. The policy required students to agree to take a drug test prior to participation, to submit to random drug testing while involved in the activity, and to be tested at any time when reasonable suspicion existed. The Court upheld the policy in light of the national increase in drug use and of increased use in the particular school. However, courts do not support the random, suspicionless drug testing of all students, but will uphold testing individual students suspected of using drugs.

Can Teachers Be Tested for Drug Use?

The Sixth Circuit Court, in 1998, upheld the suspicionless drug testing of *teachers.*[11] A Tennessee school district enacted a policy that required drug testing of applicants and employees in "safety sensitive" positions, including administrators, teachers, secretaries, aides, and bus drivers. The policy also allowed the drug testing of any employee if there was reasonable suspicion that the employee was using illegal drugs. The appeals court said, "we can imagine few governmental interests more important to a community than that of insuring the safety and security of its children while they are entrusted to the care of teachers and administrators."

Other courts have not gone this far in interpreting "safety sensitive" positions and require individualized suspicion before they can require a drug test of a teacher. A teacher was dismissed when she refused to undergo a drug test when a trained dog alerted to the odors arising from her car.[12]

We can expect new cases related to the search of teachers and other school employees regarding what constitutes individualized suspicion sufficient to warrant drug testing.

Guidelines

Due Process

- The Fourteenth Amendment applies to public schools and requires that due process be provided before teachers or students are deprived of their property rights.

- Where states provide public schools, students have a property right to attend.

- Even a short-term suspension of one to ten days must be preceded by some modicum of due process wherein students are informed of the violation and the possible punishment. They have a right to an explanation of the evidence against them, and an opportunity to refute the charges before an impartial decision maker (such as the school principal).

- A long-term suspension or expulsion must be preceded by more careful and meticulous due process, including a written notice of the charges and the intended punishment; time and place of the hearing; full and fair hearing before an impartial tribunal; right to be represented by counsel, parent, or guardian; right to know the evidence to be used against them; right to cross-examine witnesses; right to present evidence; written record of the decision and evidence it is based on; and a right to appeal.

- Students who bring drugs, guns, or other weapons to schools can be suspended and even expelled for at least a year under provisions of the No Child Left Behind Act of 2003.

- Students who are violent and present an imminent threat to themselves or others can be suspended immediately with due process to follow as soon as practicable.

- For the myriad of minor disciplinary infractions that do not lead to suspensions, no due process is required by the Fourteenth Amendment.

- Reasonable corporal punishment may be used in schools where state law, regulation, or local policy do not forbid it.

- Excessive corporal punishment may result in a criminal charge of assault and battery, in a civil suit for money damages, and in disciplinary action of suspension or dismissal.

Search and Seizure

- The Fourth Amendment protects students against unreasonable search and seizure.

- School officials may search students' cars, desks, purses, and pockets if they have reasonable suspicion that dangerous or illegal substances are hidden there. The search must be reasonable initially and in scope.

- A body search, which is highly invasive of one's privacy, must be based on probable cause.

- If police are only helping school administrators, the same standards apply. If the police are gathering evidence to be used in criminal proceedings, they must have a warrant.

- Trained dogs may be used to detect drugs in cars, lockers, and objects. The dogs' behavior may lead to a search, but not a strip search.

- Students participating in interscholastic athletics and in extracurricular activities can be required to sign a waiver permitting random, suspicionless drug testing.

- School boards can also create a policy that requires urinalysis of applicants for teaching or of teachers where there is an individualized suspicion of drug use.

- In sum, the law has been evolving to protect the due process rights of students and teachers while, at the same time, respecting the authority of school boards, teachers, and administrators to provide schooling in an orderly and safe environment.

Notes

1. *Goss v. Lopez*, 419 U.S. 565 (1975).
2. *Bethel Sch. Dist. No. 403 v. Fraser*, 478 U.S. 675 (1968).
3. 430 U.S. 651 (1977).
4. *Hall v. Tawney*, 621 F.2d 607 (4th Cir. 1980).
5. 469 U.S. 325 (1985).
6. *Horton v. Goose Creek Indep. Sch. Dist.*, 690 F.2d 470 (5th Cir. 1982).
7. *Williams v. Ellington*, 936 F.2d 881 (6th Cir. 1991).
8. *Cornfield v. Consol. High Sch. Dist. No. 230*, 991 F.2d 1316 (7th Cir. 1993).
9. *Vernonia v. Acton*, 515 U.S. 646 (1995).
10. *Bd. of Educ. v. Earls*, 536 U.S. 822 (2002).
11. *Knox County Educ. Ass'n. v. Knox Cnty. Bd. of Educ.*, 158 F.3d 361 (1998).
12. *Hearn v. Bd. of Pub. Educ.*, 191 F.3d 1329 (11th Cir. 1999).

chapter 7

Religion and Public Education

T he first publicly supported schools in America were established due to religious motives in 1647, when the Massachusetts legislature enacted the famous "old Deluder Satan" Act. The act required the establishment and support of schools in towns of 50 or more families to teach children to read and write. A person could achieve salvation and delude Satan only by being able to read the Bible. This was a Protestant conviction, and thus our earliest schools were Protestant institutions. Later in our history, Catholics, Jews, and other religious groups established their own schools since the public schools were transfused by Protestant beliefs and practices.

First Amendment Issues

How Does the Constitution Apply to Public Schools?

The First Amendment, enacted in 1791, specified that "Congress shall make no law respecting the establishment of religion, or prohibiting the free exercise thereof. . . ." Since most schooling is controlled by state and local laws and policies, how can the First Amendment restriction on Congress apply to public schools? The Supreme Court resolved this issue in the early part of the twentieth century when it held that the fundamental concept of "liberty" embodied in the Fourteenth Amendment incorporates the guarantees of the First Amendment and safeguards them against state interference.[1]

Since education is primarily a state function, even when states delegate most responsibilities to local governments, controversies involving public schools are litigated under the Fourteenth Amendment. Most of the law in this area has been established since World War II and is still evolving, particularly as the religious clauses interact with the free speech and press guarantees of the same amendment.

How Has the Establishment Clause Been Interpreted?

Everson v. Board of Education[2] was the first major establishment clause decision, wherein the Court held that the government cannot aid any one religion or even all religions, but instead must be neutral toward religion. The Court decision quoted Thomas Jefferson, who wrote that the clause was intended to erect a "wall of separation between church and state."

The "wall of separation" metaphor was used by judges for more than 30 years and, in 1971, the Supreme Court announced a three-part test to evaluate establishment clause claims in *Lemon v. Kurtzman*.[3] The government action or policy must (1) have a secular purpose, (2) have a primary effect that neither advances nor impedes religion, and (3) avoid excessive entanglement of government with religion. This tripartite test was used consistently until 1992, after which some justices expressed dissatisfaction with it and searched for another test. A majority of justices appear to favor an *endorsement standard,* under which a policy or action would be struck down if an objective person would view it as having a purpose or effect of endorsing or disapproving religion. A few favor the *coercion test,* which only prohibits government action that directly or indirectly coerces individuals to profess a faith. The current Court seems to draw on various tests depending on the facts of each case. Similarly, lower courts review governmental policies or actions under each of these tests.

What Is the Implication of the Free Exercise Clause?

In free exercise cases, individuals claim that some government actions interfere with their right to exercise their religion. To evaluate such claims, the courts apply a balancing test; that is, whether the exercise of some sincere and legitimate religious belief is impeded by a governmental action or policy and to what extent. If there is such obstruction, the court asks if there is a *compelling state interest* to justify the burden placed on the exercise of the religious belief. Even if such a compelling interest is found, the court will ask whether there is a less burdensome way to achieve the government's objective.

The best-known case involving a free exercise claim involved the Amish, where, in *Wisconsin v. Yoder,* the Court exempted the children from school attendance after successful completion of eighth grade.[4] The Court recognized education as the most important function of a state, yet balancing it against the legitimate 300-year-old religious practices of the Amish, the Court came down in favor of the children, outweighing the state's mandate of two additional years of schooling. The Court noted that the religious, close-knit agrarian way of life was unique, and it is not likely to reach a similar decision regarding other religions.

If an establishment clause violation is found, the unconstitutional government policy or practice must cease. However, if government action was found to impair the free exercise clause, the policy or program would not have to be eliminated as long as an accommodation may be made to enable individuals to practice their beliefs. For example, although the schools cannot sponsor religious programs, students may form prayer groups and meet during noninstructional times to pray or read the Bible or other religious works.

There is an interesting tension between claims under the free exercise and establishment clauses, so controversies will continue to arise. During recent years, this area of the law has become further complicated when free speech claims have been introduced related to religious content. Recent developments of claims based on free speech in school-related matters with religious content have made the work of the courts much more complicated.

Prayer and Bible Reading in Public Schools

Historically, the day in public schools began with a prayer, Bible reading, and some patriotic exercise. It was in the early 1960s that the Supreme Court declared that school-sponsored prayer and/or Bible reading violated the establishment clause.[5] Similarly, the Sixth Circuit Court held unconstitutional the practice of opening school board meetings with a prayer.

May Students Pray Silently in School?

More recent controversies have focused on state laws or school policies encouraging or allowing silent prayers in public schools. The Supreme Court struck down an Alabama law in 1985 that inserted the phrase "or voluntary prayer" into an existing statute that authorized a period of silent meditation. The insertion indicated an intent to encourage students to pray. Without such a legislative intent, the Court would have upheld the law.[6]

Many states have laws that provide for a moment of silence for prayer or meditation. These laws have been upheld in a variety of lawsuits where there is no clear evidence that the intent behind them was to encourage students to pray in school. It has been held that a moment of silence at the start of a school day is a constitutional way to settle the students.

A more recent highly controversial issue centers around student-initiated and -conducted devotionals in public schools. Cases have been litigated concerning student-led prayers at sport events, graduation exercises, and other school activities. Generally, courts declared these unconstitutional if clergy were involved or if obviously religious messages were to be conveyed.

Are Graduation Prayers Permitted?

It has been a common practice for principals to invite members of the clergy to deliver invocations and benedictions at graduation ceremonies. In *Lee v. Weisman,* such a policy in a Rhode Island school district was declared unconstitutional by the Court as a violation of the establishment clause.[7] Though attendance was voluntary, the Court considered that students would feel coercive peer pressure to attend such an important school-sponsored event.

Many school districts found "clever" ways to circumvent the *Weisman* decision. Some school districts designated the graduation ceremony a "forum for student expression" and students could include religious messages at their discretion. An Idaho school district, for example, selected student speakers by class standing and allowed them to recite "an address, poem, reading, song, musical presentation, prayer, or any other pronouncement of their choosing."[8] The Ninth Circuit Court upheld the school policy that prohibited school authorities from censoring the students' speeches. The court considered the ceremony to be a forum for student expression, where the speakers had been selected on secular criteria, and had not been advised to include devotionals in their remarks.

In other cases, where school authorities maintained control over graduation ceremonies, they could censor proposed religious speeches in order to avoid
violating the establishment clause. Another way to avoid constitutional conflicts
would be for students, churches, or other private groups to rent space and conduct
baccalaureate graduation ceremonies that include prayers. If public schools are in
no way involved, there is no "state action" and therefore no violation of the establishment clause.[9]

What about Student Prayer Clubs?

A federal statute, the Equal Access Act, also makes it possible for secondary
school students to meet voluntarily, before or after school or during their lunch
hour, to worship or discuss religion if other extracurricular groups are permitted. These meetings must be student-organized and led without the involvement
of teachers or outsiders. Teachers may be present but only to enforce proper
discipline.

Can Students Be Required to Recite the Pledge of Allegiance or Salute the Flag?

No. The Supreme Court made it clear in 1943 in *West Virginia v. Barnette*[10] that
students may not be required to salute the flag. In an oft-quoted statement, Justice
Jackson wrote for the majority:

> If there is any fixed star in our constitutional constellation, it is that no official,
> high or petty, can prescribe what shall be orthodox in politics, nationalism, reli-
> gion, or other matters of opinion or force citizens to confess by word or act their
> faith therein. If there are any circumstances which permit an exception, they do not
> now occur to us.

Consistent with *Barnette,* both students and teachers may be excused from saluting
the flag if they object to it on the basis of religion or conscience. If state law requires a daily flag salute, however, teachers must make some provision that it will
take place, whether led by a class officer, another teacher, or a cooperating parent.
Students who object to the pledge may not disrupt it but can remain in the room in
respectful silence. They may not be required to stand or to leave the room.

The inclusion of the phrase "under God" probably does not violate the establishment clause, although there is no authoritative Supreme Court decision
on this matter. The only case that has reached the Court so far, *Newdow v. United
States,*[11] was dismissed on procedural grounds because the father who brought

the suit did not have legal custody of the student. Some future case will have to address this issue.

Can Schools Sponsor Religious Displays, Symbols, and Programs?

The establishment clause requirement that schools must be neutral concerning religion has led to various challenges of religious displays, symbols, and holiday observances in schools. In 1985, the Supreme Court declared a Kentucky law unconstitutional that required the posting of the Ten Commandments in public school classrooms.[12] Lower courts have also found objectionable the display of religious paintings in schools, but have allowed the recognition of religious holidays on school calendars as a way of developing students' knowledge of religion in history.

Courts are likely to strike down religious displays, symbols, or programs that are sectarian or are likely to advance religion. On the other hand, those that are educational and objective presentations of our nation's diversity or historical development are likely to be upheld by our courts.

Classroom teachers must also take care that their clothing, instructional program, or classroom displays do not suggest an effort to proselytize students. The Supreme Court, however, clearly upheld the use of the Bible and other religious materials to teach *about* religion and its role in history and culture, but not to promote religion.

Distribution of religious materials has also arisen as a controversial issue. The Supreme Court has not addressed this matter and lower courts have rendered various opinions. Schools cannot give students such materials and most courts have prevented religious groups from doing so. The Fourth Circuit upheld a West Virginia school district policy that allowed religious groups, along with political groups, to distribute materials in secondary schools, but not in elementary schools, where students are more impressionable. If students request to distribute religious materials, the courts tend to apply the "equal access" test to religious and nonreligious materials.

How Can Schools Accommodate Students' Religious Beliefs?

Historically, schools have often set aside time in school, during school hours, for religious instruction. This practice was declared unconstitutional in 1948,[13] leading to "release-time" religious education, where the instruction took place off school grounds. This arrangement was upheld in 1952,[14] and it is practiced in many school districts even today. While this accommodation is legal, many teachers find that it disrupts their planned instructional programs.

Both teachers and students have a right to be excused from school attendance to observe religious holidays. Such absences must be reasonable in number.

Students may also secure exemption on religious grounds from sex education, drug education, coeducational physical education, dancing, and officers' training programs. The burden of proof is on the parents to show that their sincerely held religious beliefs would be violated by the curriculum offering. In the most famous case in this area, the parents were unsuccessful in their attempt to have their children excused from reading a basal reading series in the elementary schools in a Tennessee school district.[15] The appeals court found no burden on the students' religious beliefs since they were not required to perform religious exercises or profess belief. Parents at times object to portions of a "health curriculum." Courts might exempt students from parts of such curriculum, usually "sex education," but not from the entire program.

What about Religious Challenges to the Curriculum?

In addition to requests to be excused from sex education, there have been many challenges to teaching about Darwin's theory of evolution. While the famous Scopes "monkey trial" upheld the antievolution law of Tennessee, the U.S. Supreme Court struck down an Arkansas antievolution statute under the establishment clause, holding that evolution theory is a science and a state cannot restrict such teaching in favor of a religious preference.[16] Efforts to secure equal time for teaching about "creationism" and "intelligent design" with teaching about evolution have met similar defeat in the courts.

Parents have also tried unsuccessfully to exclude certain reading series for promoting witchcraft or Satanism—the most recent of such challenges focusing on the *Harry Potter* series. However, one New York case ruled in favor of parents who asserted that parts of a program offended their Catholic faith.[17] A requirement that students construct images of a Hindu deity violated the First Amendment, and the making of worry dolls was prohibited because it indicated a preference for superstition over religion in violation of the establishment clause.

Ever new controversies come to the courts that require interpretations of the establishment and free exercise clauses of the First Amendment. The foregoing are the ones of most direct relevance to teachers and students, though there are many others that relate to school finance, aid to private schools, and other issues school boards must address from time to time. The changing composition of the Supreme Court will also influence the evolution of the law in this highly controversial area.

Guidelines

- The establishment clause and free exercise clause of the First Amendment are the constitutional principles that control the relationship between religion and public schools.

- Public schools must be neutral toward religion. They may neither favor a religion or all religions nor be hostile toward religion.

- The Fourteenth Amendment incorporates the First Amendment's protection of basic rights and applies them to the states.

- Since public schooling is a state function, actions of teachers, administrators, and school boards are "state actions" for purposes of constitutional law and therefore the Fourteenth Amendment applies to them.

- Most school-related litigation concerning religion has involved the establishment clause, although some recent cases concern claims under the free exercise clause as well.

- Earlier cases relied heavily on Thomas Jefferson's famous "wall of separation" metaphor, but more recent cases also use the Lemon test, the coercion test or the endorsement test.

- The free speech clause has become increasingly important in protecting "religious speech" in schools along with the protection of student religious activities during noninstructional time.

- Neither students nor teachers can be required to recite the Pledge of Allegiance or salute the flag, if they object on the grounds of religion or conscience.

- Teachers who object to the Pledge of Allegiance or saluting the flag must make provisions to carry on these activities if required by state law.

- Holiday programs may take place in schools if they have a secular educational purpose and do not create a religious atmosphere.

- The display of the Ten Commandments, religious pictures, symbols, and pageants in schools violate the principal of neutrality.

- Parents or church groups may not distribute religious materials in school. Students, however, may do so if it does not interfere with school activities or create substantial disruption.

- School-sponsored prayers or religious speeches are unconstitutional at graduation exercises.

- Prayers at school athletic events are unconstitutional since they give the impression that schools are sponsoring the religious activity.
- Schools must be continually on guard not to violate the principle of neutrality in this highly sensitive area.

Notes

1. *Gitlow v. New York,* 268 U.S. 652 (1925); *Cantwell v. Connecticut,* 310 U.S. 296 (1940).
2. *Everson v. Bd. of Educ.,* 330 U.S. 1 (1947).
3. *Lemon v. Kurtzman,* 403 U.S. 602 (1971).
4. *Wisconsin v. Yoder,* 406 U.S. 502 (1972).
5. *Engle v. Vitale,* 370 U.S. 421 (1962); *Sch. Dist. of Abington Township v. Schemp,* 374 U.S. 203 (1963).
6. *Wallace v. Jaffee,* 472 U.S. 38 (1985).
7. *Lee v. Weisman,* 505 U.S. 577 (1992).
8. *Doe v. Madison Sch. Dist. No 321,* 147 F.2d 832 (9th Cir. 1998), *vacated and remanded en banc* (because the student had graduated).
9. *Lassonde v. Pleasanton Unified Sch. Dist.,* 320 F.3d 979 (9th Cir. 2003).
10. *West Virginia v. Barnette,* 319 U.S. 624 (1943).
11. *Newdow v. United States,* 542 U.S. 1 (2004).
12. *Stone v. Graham,* 449 U.S. 39 (1980).
13. *McCollum v. Bd. of Educ.,* 333 U.S. 203 (1948).
14. *Zorach v. Clausen,* 343 U.S. 306 (1952).
15. *Mozert v. Hawkins Cnty. Bd. of Educ.,* 827 F.2d 1058 (6th Cir. 1987).
16. *Epperson v. Arkansas,* 393 U.S. 97 (1968).
17. *Altman v. Bedford Cent. Sch. Dist.,* 245 F.3d 49 (. 827 (2001).

chapter 8

Discrimination and Equal Protection

Race, Gender, Age, Language, and Special Education

Ever since schools existed, students have been grouped using various criteria. During recent decades, there have been significant court cases challenging the constitutionality of classifying students based on race, gender, native language, age, and disability. Discrimination against teachers using these criteria has also been challenged in courts.

Classification by Race

Historically, our public schools have been segregated by race. In our southern states, segregation was mandated by state constitutions or statutes, while in the north it resulted from residential segregation. Residential segregation was brought about by economic discrimination, real estate "redlining," the policies of banks and mortgage companies, and deed restrictions. Residential segregation coupled with neighborhood schools, particularly when local school boards drew attendance lines, substantially ensured segregated schooling in our northern communities as well.

Did the Equal Protection Clause of the Fourteenth Amendment Eliminate Segregated Schooling?

Initially it did not. Since the broad language of the Constitution needs to be interpreted, the Supreme Court was called on to determine the meaning of the equal protection clause, as applied to schooling. In the famous case of *Plessy v. Ferguson*[1] in 1896, the Court announced the doctrine of "separate but equal." Although *Plessy* involved segregation in public transportation required by Louisiana law, three years later the Court applied the same principle to the education of public school children.

Despite a variety of challenges to the *Plessy* doctrine over a half a century, it was not overturned until 1954, when, in *Brown v. Board of Education,*[2] the Supreme Court declared that segregated public schools were "inherently unequal." The following year, in *Brown II,*[3] the Court ordered schools to desegregate "with all deliberate speed."

How Speedily Did School Districts Carry Out the Court's Mandate?

Very slowly. Massive foot-dragging, subterfuge, and occasional violence delayed desegregation nationwide, and it took almost another half a century for public schools to desegregate in the North and South as well as the East and West. And vestiges of segregated schooling may still be found in some communities.

The *Green*[4] case from Virginia specified six factors for judges to consider in determining whether a school system has eliminated segregation. These became known as the *Green Criteria* and are still used today. The six factors are the composition of the student body, the faculty, staff, facilities, transportation, and extracurricular activities. The Supreme Court has also pronounced that the days of "deliberate speed" are over, all schools must get rid of racial segregation, and the only desegregation plan that is constitutional is one that works.

What about Communities Where Resegregation Occurs?

The Fourteenth Amendment only outlaws segregation that results from the law, school board policy, or actions of institutions licensed by the state. Such segregation is *de jure,* as contrasted with *de facto* (as a matter of fact) segregation where no official acts were involved. Thus, if a school district has no history of *de jure* segregation or if it achieves a unitary status (a desegregated status), and afterward, with no official action but as a result of population mobility, it becomes segregated or resegregated, that is *de facto* segregation and does not violate the Constitution.[5]

Who Supervises the Process of Desegregation?

The federal district court closest to the school district involved in the litigation has continuous jurisdiction until desegregation is complete and a unitary district is achieved. This might take a short time, but it could take more than 20 or 30 years, as it did in Boston and Los Angeles. Once such unitary status is achieved, the federal district court can terminate its supervision if it is satisfied that the district will not return to its former discriminating ways and has complied with all court orders in good faith to the extent practicable.[6] It is also possible to relinquish court supervision over those portions of the district's operation that satisfied the court's orders while the district continues its efforts to satisfy the rest under continued court supervision.[7]

Are Teachers Protected against Racial Discrimination?

Yes, they are protected by the Fourteenth Amendment and by Title VII of the Civil Rights Act of 1964. The Fourteenth Amendment mandates that no state shall deny to any person within its jurisdiction equal protection of the laws. And Title VII prohibits employers, both public and private, with 15 or more employees from discriminating on the basis of race, color, religion, gender, or national origin. Title VII covers hiring, promotion, and compensation practices and other terms and conditions of employment.

Both disparate treatment and disparate impact are prohibited by the statute. *Disparate treatment* occurs when an individual is the victim of discrimination, whereas *disparate impact* occurs when an individual's class has been discriminated against because of the discriminating impact of a neutral policy or practice.[8]

An applicant for a teaching position who claims discrimination based on disparate treatment has to show that he or she is a member of a protected class, is qualified for the job, was denied the position, and that the employer continued to look for applicants with the same qualifications. To claim discrimination based on disparate impact, one must show that the employer's apparently neutral policy or practice had a disproportionate impact on one's protected class. If a teacher succeeds in showing this, the school district must show that the policy or practice is job related and justified by a business necessity. Title VII also protects employees against retaliation for having filed complaints or suits for discrimination.

Can School Districts Hire on the Basis of Race or Ethnicity?

Only under special circumstances. It is not sufficient that a school district may want to hire minority teachers or administrators to provide role models for its students. They may engage in such hiring if there has been a proven history of discrimination in the district. Without past discrimination, race or ethnicity cannot be a major consideration in personnel decisions. However, if there has been a proven history of discrimination, the court will determine the appropriate remedy that will overcome the vestiges of prior unconstitutional actions. Similarly, negative personnel decisions must not be tainted by unconstitutional considerations of race or ethnicity but must be based on the employee's job performance.

Can School Districts Use Affirmative Action to Hire Teachers or in the Placement of Students?

Only in rare circumstances. Affirmative action is defined by the U.S. Commission on Civil Rights as "steps to be taken to remedy the grossly disparate staffing and recruitment patterns that are the present consequences of past discrimination and to prevent the occurrence of employment discrimination in the future."

In sum, constitutional and statutory protections are now available to overcome the vestiges of past racial discrimination in education. Whether public schools can use affirmative action to achieve racial balance among students is a controversy now before the Supreme Court.

Gender Discrimination against Teachers

Although the overwhelming majority of teachers are women, they are the subjects of most cases of gender discrimination. Today, most forms of such discrimination are prohibited by law. The Fourteenth Amendment and Title VII are the key legal resources with which to fight gender discrimination.

Can Gender Be Used in Hiring Teachers?

In general no, unless there is a legitimate occupational qualification for a male or female, for example, the supervising of girls' or boys' locker rooms. To advertise for a male art teacher or a female kindergarten teacher is obvious gender discrimination. On the other hand, a seemingly neutral recruiting process might result in the exclusion of female applicants; for example, an advertisement for head counselor for boys. In such a situation, business necessity might be a justification.

An employer may always justify a hiring decision by showing that the successful candidate was better qualified than the others. Some gender-based distinctions are also allowed by Title VII as bona fide occupational qualification (BFOQ) exceptions.

Can Pay Differentials Be Based on Gender?

Not if male and female teachers are equally qualified in terms of degrees held and years of experience. Some school districts also give credit for years of military service or civil service classification.

In the past, males often received higher pay for being a "head of household"; now, however, such a pay differential must also be available to women if they are heads of households. The Equal Pay Act of 1963 also applies to gender-based wage discrimination claims of unequal pay for equal work. To determine whether the jobs in question are equal, courts look at the nature of the required tasks as well as the efforts, responsibilities, skills, and working conditions associated with the jobs.

Gender may not be a factor in other personnel decisions, such as reappointment, promotion, or tenure. An employee claiming discrimination must prove intent to discriminate by the employer. This is often very difficult to do unless the administrator or some member of the board made some careless remarks.

Is Discrimination Based on Pregnancy or Childbirth Allowable?

No. It is forbidden by the Pregnancy Discrimination Act,[9] which makes it illegal to refuse to hire an otherwise qualified applicant because of pregnancy. Employers may not even inquire about applicants' intentions to have children, or how the children will be cared for if applicants are hired.

If the employer requires a physician's statement about the medical condition of an applicant or an employee, it may also require one for pregnancy prior to granting a leave or paying medical benefits. If a pregnant employee is unable to perform her job due to pregnancy, she must be treated as any other temporarily disabled person. If she decides to take a leave, her position must be held open in the same manner as if she were sick or otherwise disabled. Furthermore, the historic practice of requiring pregnant teachers to take a leave of absence prior to the birth of a child and specifying a date when they may return was struck down by the Supreme Court as a violation of the due process clause[10] because it creates an *irrebuttable presumption* that all pregnant teachers are physically unable to work as of a specified date.

Gender Discrimination against Students

Our earliest schools were for males only. Schools merely reflected the widespread discrimination against women in the culture at large. When girls were finally allowed to enroll in schools, their schooling was usually segregated and inferior. It took many years and much controversy to achieve substantial equality in schooling free of gender discrimination. Major breakthroughs occurred only in the latter part of the twentieth century, with the aid of the Fourteenth Amendment and Title IX of the Education Amendments of 1972.

Athletic activities and competition were important parts of the education of boys going back to ancient Greece. Girls were merely spectators and, in more recent times, cheerleaders. This began to change with compulsory schooling when physical education was required of all children attending school.

Is Gender Discrimination in Sport Competition Permissible?

Title IX allows public schools to have separate teams for each sex. However, where schools have a team for one sex but not for the other, members of the excluded sex must be able to try out for the team offered unless it is a contact sport such as football or basketball.[11]

A highly controversial issue related to high school athletics is the participation of boys and girls together in a contact sport. Title IX does not require gender segregation in contact sports, though it permits it. Each school may determine for itself whether it can meet the goal of equal athletic opportunity through separate or coeducational teams. Regional athletic associations often have rules forbidding coeducational competition; however, it is still up to each school to decide whether to field coeducational teams.

A New York case ruled on the basis of the Fourteenth Amendment that a female junior high student had a right to try out for the junior varsity football squad. The school failed to show that its policy against mixed competition served an important governmental objective. When the school claimed that the policy was to protect the health and safety of female students, the court indicated that female students were not given an opportunity to show that they were as strong and fit as the weakest male member of the team.[12] A Wisconsin case ruled similarly.[13] States with state Equal Rights Amendments have also allowed mixed gender athletic competition.[14]

Are Single-Sex Public Schools Legal?

The federal Education Department announced on October 25, 2006, that public schools may create single-sex schools and classes as long as enrollment in them is voluntary. School districts that create such single-sex schools must make available coeducational schools and classes of "substantially equal" quality available for students of the excluded sex.[15]

In 1977, a federal appeals court upheld a gender-segregated high school in Philadelphia.[16] The court found that the education was substantially equal in the two schools and attendance was voluntary. The court accepted the argument that adolescents might study more effectively in gender-separated institutions, and the female plaintiff had the option of attending a coeducational school within her attendance zone.

Philadelphia has had such single-sex schools available for years and plans to open more of them. Nationwide, the number of single-sex public schools for girls or boys has risen from 3 in 1995 to 241 in 2006, according to the National Association for Single-Sex Schools. New York City has nine such schools.

Although research related to the effectiveness of single-sex schools is equivocal, Secretary of Education Margaret Spellings claims that such schools expand educational options in public schooling. Some women's groups and some civil rights groups are considering challenging the 2006 change as reinstituting official discrimination in schools around the country in violation of Title IX.

A proposal to open and operate all-male schools for African American students in Detroit, with a unique Afrocentric curriculum, was disallowed by a federal district court.[17] There was no equivalent school for girls except as a promise in the future. The court held that the proposal violated the equal protection clause, Title IX, and the state law.

Can School Districts Compel Pregnant Students to Transfer to a Separate School?

No. Under regulations promulgated by the U.S. Department of Education under Title IX, schools may not discriminate against an enrolled student in academic or nonacademic activities because of pregnancy, birth of a child, false pregnancy, miscarriage, or termination of pregnancy unless the student opts to participate in a comparable alternative activity. Requiring a pregnant student to attend a school exclusively for pregnant women would constitute a form of segregation and discrimination.

Sexual Harassment of Teachers

Sexual harassment refers to repeated unwelcome sexual advances, sexually suggestive speech, or sexually offensive gestures or acts. Both men and women can be victims of sexual harassment from persons of the opposite or same sex. Under Title VII, two types of sexual harassment have been identified: quid pro quo and hostile environment.

Quid pro quo means giving something for something. To establish such a claim, a plaintiff must show that she or he was subjected to unwelcome sexual advances and requests for sexual favors; the harassment was based on gender; and submission was an express or implied condition for a favorable action, such as promotion, or avoidance of some adverse action by the employer or supervisor.

In a suit based on the theory of hostile environment, a plaintiff must show that the workplace environment is severely or pervasively hostile so as to unreasonably interfere with the person's work performance. The plaintiff also must show that the sexually offensive conduct was unwelcome and the harasser was informed of that fact.

School districts should have sexual harassment policies that are disseminated to all employees. Supervisory personnel should be trained to understand and follow these policies. Grievance procedures should be available for reporting harassment. Timely corrective action must be taken.

Sexual Harassment of Students

The Fourteenth Amendment and Title IX both apply to claims of sexual harassment of students. The Supreme Court ruled that, for a student to collect money damages from the district for harassment by a teacher, a school official with authority to address the alleged discrimination must have had actual knowledge of the inappropriate conduct and failed to address the problem. Furthermore, the school official had to act with "deliberate indifference" in responding or not responding to such discrimination.[18]

Can Students Sue Schools for Harassment by Other Students?

Yes, they can if the harassment is severe, pervasive, and objectively offensive so as to prevent the victim from having access to educational opportunity. The school officials would have to have knowledge of the harassment and acted with deliberate indifference. The Supreme Court so ruled in 1999 in *Davis v. Monroe County Board of Education* where a school failed to take any action to stop lewd comments and unwelcome touching despite repeated complaints for more than three months.[19]

Discrimination Based on Age

How Does Age Discrimination Affect School Employees?

Employees receive protection against age discrimination under the Fourteenth Amendment and under the Age Discrimination in Employment Act (ADEA).[20] The ADEA applies to employees aged 40 or older who work in a place with 20 or more employees. The act applies to failure to hire or to discharge persons, or otherwise discriminate in compensation or terms and conditions of their employment because of their age. An ADEA violation might result in the employer being compelled to hire, reinstate, or promote the plaintiff with compensation for back pay, damages, and attorney fees.

Age discrimination in hiring is difficult to prove, because an employer has discretion to select a better-qualified person. Plaintiffs who challenge an adverse employment action must show they were 40 or older; applied for and were qualified for the position; were subject to a negative decision; and a younger person took their place. An involuntary transfer to a lesser position because of age would have to be challenged in the same way.

How Does Age Discrimination Affect Students?

State laws generally require students to attend school between the ages of 6 and 16. In many states, they may attend between the ages of 3 and 21.

There have been a variety of cases involving students with disabilities who were overaged and wanted to participate in interscholastic sports in violation of the rules specified by regional scholastic athletic associations. Often, sport participation is included in the disabled student's IEP. Courts have arrived at conflicting decisions in these cases, so there is no uniform law on this subject.

English Language Learners

May Schools Discriminate against Students of Limited English Proficiency?

No, they may not. Their rights are protected by the Fourteenth Amendment, Title VI of the Civil Rights Act of 1964, and the Equal Educational Opportunity Act of 1974 (EEOA). The No Child Left Behind Act also addresses the rights of limited English-speaking students.

The best-known case, and only Supreme Court case, addressing this issue arose in San Francisco, where instruction in English was provided for non-English-speaking students who were recent immigrants from China. The Court ruled that such education, in the absence of adequate remedial instruction in English, violated Title VI.[21] The Court wrote that "basic English skills are the very core of what these public schools teach . . . students who do not understand English are effectively foreclosed from any meaningful education."

Because there are scholarly disagreements about the best way to educate students with limited English proficiency (LEP), the courts do not require any one method to be used. In fact, the federal law no longer uses the term *bilingual education,* but speaks of limited English proficiency students. In different states, school districts have used a variety of programs and, if they do so in good faith, with reasonable results, courts will approve their programs. This was the case in Berkeley, California, where a Spanish bilingual program and three forms of English as a Second Language programs were approved by the court.[22] California also passed Proposition 227, which requires that "nearly all" instruction be in English using "Sheltered English immersion" (SEI) methods and procedures. The law exempts children who already possess good English skills. When challenged by the California Teachers' Association as too vague, the circuit court upheld the law.[23]

In sum, federal laws protect limited English proficiency students against discrimination and allow schools to use various methods that in good faith try to overcome language disabilities of students.

Special Education

Can Schools Discriminate against Students with Disabilities?

No, they cannot, although historically there was widespread exclusion of disabled children from schools as well as substantial educational neglect when they were enrolled. In recent years, a number or lawsuits inspired some important legislation that has significantly changed this area of schooling.

How Has the *Brown* Case Helped Disabled Children?

Although the *Brown v. Board of Education* case was about racial segregation, the language of the Supreme Court emphasized that education is perhaps the most important function of the state and that it "must be made available to all on equal terms." Ultimately, this helped the admission of disabled students to public schools. Legislation in several states as well as court cases eventually led to federal legislation originally known as the Education of Handicapped Children Act (94-142). Today, the major federal laws used to achieve equality of education for the disabled are the Individuals with Disabilities Education Act (IDEA), the Americans with Disabilities Act (ADA), and the Rehabilitation Act (Section 504).

For public education, the most important of these laws is the IDEA. This law requires that qualified children receive free appropriate public education (FAPE) in the least restrictive environment. Who are qualified for FAPE? Children who are hard of hearing, deaf, mentally impaired, speech or language impaired, blind, visually impaired, seriously emotionally disturbed, orthopedically impaired, autistic, other health-impaired, learning disabled, or suffer from traumatic brain injury, and, as a result, are in need of special education and related services.[24]

What Constitutes a Free Appropriate Public Education?

All children with disabilities, from ages 3 to 21 (except in states that do not serve ages 3 to 4 and 18 to 21), are entitled to FAPE at public expense and under public supervision. The schooling must meet the standards of the state educational agency; be in conformity with the student's individualized educational program (IEP); and include preschool, elementary, and secondary school education. The students must be provided supplementary aids and services; transition services to enable them to progress from school to postschool activities; and assistive technology devices and services to improve functional capabilities.

Must FAPE Provide Education That Will Maximize a Student's Learning Potential?

No, ruled the Supreme Court in the *Rowley* case.[25] The intent of the law was to guarantee a "basic floor of opportunity", and the evidence showed that the student was making better-than-average progress academically as well as socially. The Court indicated that lower courts should simply ask two questions: First, did the state comply with the procedures identified in the IDEA? Second, is the IEP reasonably calculated to enable the child to receive educational benefit?

What Constitutes an Individualized Educational Program?

The IDEA has a "child find" provision, pursuant to which school districts must find and evaluate all resident children with disabilities whether they attend public or private schools. Its "zero reject" provision requires that no child with a disability be denied an appropriate program.

Before a child with disabilities is placed in a program, there must be thorough evaluation by qualified personnel, using standardized tests. The evaluation must be in the child's native language and be free of racial or cultural bias. Informed consent of the parents or guardians must be secured prior to the evaluation of the child. If the parents refuse consent, the school district may secure such consent through due process procedures. If the parents disagree with the district's evaluation and placement, they have a right to request an independent evaluation.

School districts have IEP teams responsible for deciding whether a child is qualified under the IDEA for services and for designing appropriate least restrictive placement. An IEP team should include the parents of the child with the disability; at least one regular education teacher; at least one special education teacher; a district representative qualified to provide or supervise specially designed instruction to meet the unique needs of the child; other individuals who have special knowledge or expertise relevant to the child's needs; and possibly the child.

The IEP team creates a program for the child specifying annual goals and objectives; special education–related services; the extent to which the student will be included in general education activities; the date to initiate the services, together with their frequency and duration; and how the parents will be informed of the child's progress. The program must be reviewed at least annually, and a reevaluation must take place every three years if requested by the parents, the IEP team, or any of the child's teachers.

What Is the Least Restrictive Environment (LRE)?

The IDEA requires that children with disabilities be educated in the least restrictive environment; to the maximum extent appropriate, with children who are not disabled. The regulations list a continuum from a regular classroom with support services all the way to home schooling or instruction in hospitals or residential institutions.[26]

The most important consideration is the provision of an appropriate program and secondarily the placement that is the least restrictive. Such placement may be in public or private schools or institutions. If an appropriate program is available in a public school and the parent chooses a private school or facility for noneducational reasons, the parents will most likely have to bear the costs.

Must Schools Provide Year-Round Instruction for Disabled Children?

Yes, for children who regress significantly during the summer vacation and when the IEP team considers it essential for them to recoup what they would lose. The nature of the summer program is determined by the IEP team.

What Are the "Related Services" Required by the IDEA?

The act defines related services as:

> Transportation, and such developmental, corrective, and other support services (including speech pathology and audiology, psychological services, physical and occupational therapy, recreation, and medical and counseling services, except that such medical services shall be for diagnostic and evaluative purposes only) as may be required to assist the handicapped child to benefit from special education, and includes the early identification and assessment of handicapping conditions in children.[27]

The question of what are related services was a key issue in the *Tatro* case.[28] Amber Tatro, born with spina bifida, suffered from orthopedic and speech impairments and a condition that prevented her from emptying her bladder voluntarily. She had to be catheterized every 3 or 4 hours to avoid injury to her kidneys. Is such periodic catheterization during school hours a related service or an excluded medical service? "Clean intermittent catheterization" (CIC) was not included in her IEP, though it is a simple procedure that can be learned in about an hour and requires 5 minutes to administer. The Supreme Court ruled that CIC was a related service because it made it possible for the child to remain in school during the day, without which she could not be educated.

Other highly controversial cases went to courts trying to distinguish between related services and medical services not covered by IDEA. In Pennsylvania, 7-year-old Bevin had fetal face syndrome, was profoundly mentally handicapped, suffered from plastic quadriplegia and a seizure disorder, and was legally blind. She was fed and given medicine through a gastrostomy tube and breathed through a tracheostomy tube. Without a doubt, the services of a trained nurse were necessary to keep her in school.[29] Nursing services cost $1,850 a month in 1984–1985, excluding close to $1,000 additional expenses a month for Bevin outside of school. The court concluded that neither IDEA, its regulations, nor case law include such extensive and expensive nursing care under related services.

Must Schools Administer Prescription Drugs to Disabled Students?

Yes, if the medications are prescribed by the student's physician. The school nurse usually administers such medications. In one case, the physician prescribed a dosage of Ritalin larger than the recommended daily dose listed in the *Physicians' Desk Reference*. When the school refused to administer the larger dose, the parents sued. The court held that the school provided reasonable accommodation under a facially neutral policy, for it was willing to have the parents give the larger dose at school or modify the student's schedule so that the Ritalin could be given to her at home.[30]

Can Schools Discipline Children with Disabilities?

Yes, they can if their misbehavior is not a manifestation of their disabling condition and if due process is followed. Long-term suspension or expulsion, however, are considered changes in educational placement and are allowed only after procedures specified by law are followed. Under the law, appropriate alternative educational placement must be found for such students.[31]

Before a suspension of 10 or more days, or an expulsion, there must be a "manifestation determination" review. At a meeting conducted by representatives of the local educational agency, the parents and certain members of the IEP team determine whether the offending behavior was a manifestation of the disability. If it was, standard disciplinary procedures will not be applied to the student, and the IEP team must develop a plan to address the behavior or alter the existing plan. These changes went into effect in 2005 and must be consistent with the No Child Left Behind Act. At a subsequent meeting, a *behavior intervention plan* must be developed by the IEP team, together with the student's regular teacher and any other qualified personnel. The team may recommend a change of placement (COP), which the parents may accept or challenge.

A 1997 amendment to the IDEA provides legal protection for students not yet eligible for special education who are facing possible expulsion. The amendment allows the parents of such children to request protection under the IDEA by alleging that school personnel knew or should have known that the student had a disability before the misconduct occurred that triggered the disciplinary process. When such a request is made and there are some reasonable grounds for it, the "stay-put" provision of IDEA mandates that the student not be expelled, but an IEP team should determine the student's eligibility for special education and all its procedural safeguards.

Can Students Whose Behavior Is Dangerous Be Given Long-Term Suspension?

Not according to the Supreme Court's 1988 ruling in *Honig Doe.*[32] Doe, a 17-year-old special education student whose IEP explicitly recognized his propensity for aggressive acts, acted explosively when taunted by a fellow student. He "choked the student with sufficient force to leave abrasions" on the neck and "kicked out a school window" while being escorted to the principal's office afterward. When the school proceeded with a summary long-term suspension, suit was filed on behalf of Doe. The school district claimed that the IDEA implicitly contained a "dangerousness exception" to the "stay-put" provision. However, the Supreme Court disagreed and said that "the stay-put provision was intended to remove the unilateral authority school officials traditionally exercised to exclude disabled children, particularly emotionally disabled children, from school." School officials, however, may temporarily suspend dangerous students for up to 10 days, can initiate a review of their IEP, and work with the parents to agree on an interim placement. If the parents refuse to permit any change in placement, the 10-day period gives school officials an opportunity to ask the courts to approve a new placement.

A 1997 amendment to the IDEA enables school officials to place a student with dangerous drugs or weapons in an "interim alternative setting" for 45 days. The student must be allowed to continue to receive IEP services to reduce the risk of future dangerous behavior.

Can High-Stakes Tests Be Used with Students with Disabilities?

This question was raised by many students under a variety of laws. The 1997 amendment to the IDEA requires state and local education agencies to develop guidelines to enable children with disabilities to participate in state or district assessments. The student's IEP must describe the modifications to be made to enable the student to participate in the assessment. If, on the other hand, the IEP team decides that a student should not participate, it should state its reasons and how the student will be assessed.

As the law now stands, "high-stakes testing," when following the provisions of IDEA, giving sufficient notice, and adequately presenting the relevant curriculum, does not violate the law even if some students with disabilities are thereby prevented from receiving a diploma. Disabled students in California challenged the requirement that they pass the California High School Exit Exam to receive a high school diploma.[33] The federal district court ruled that such requirement, without accommodations, would be injurious to the "individual dignity" of the disabled student. The court noted that the IEPs must address individual modifications for statewide assessments and guide the accommodations acceptable for taking such tests. For students unable to master the high school curriculum, alternative assessment must be provided under the IDEA.

Guidelines

Race Discrimination and Equal Protection

- The equal protection clause of the Fourteenth Amendment forbids racial segregation in schooling by law or policy, and both teachers and students are protected against racial and ethnic discrimination.
- Racial resegregation that occurs as a result of population mobility, without official action, is *de facto* segregation and does not violate the Constitution.
- School districts may hire on the basis of race only to overcome a proven history of discrimination.

Gender Discrimination and Equal Protection

- The Fourteenth Amendment, Title VII, Title IX, and state Equal Rights Amendments are the key legal resources with which to challenge gender discrimination.
- Gender may be considered in a hiring decision only if it is a legitimate occupational qualification.
- Gender cannot be used to justify a pay differential, or any personnel decision, and there can be no discrimination based on pregnancy or childbirth.

- Title IX is the principal federal law controlling the sports participation of boys and girls in public schools.

- If a school has a team in a sport for members of one sex but not for the other, and athletic opportunities for that sex have historically been limited, members of the excluded sex must be allowed to try out for the team unless the sport is a contact sport. But, in some states, those with state ERAs, they can try out for contact sports also.

- As a general rule, schools cannot have gender-separate academic programs. New regulations allow school districts to offer gender-segregated classes and schools if they are genuinely equal, and there are coed alternatives.

- Sexual harassment of teachers or students violates Title VII, independently of gender.

- Schools can be held responsible for student-on-student harassment if it was severe and pervasive, and if school officials knew about it and acted with deliberate indifference.

Discrimination Based on Age

- A federal law protects employees over 40 years of age from age discrimination in hiring, discharge, and other personnel actions.

Students with Limited English Proficiency

- Students with limited English proficiency are protected by the Fourteenth Amendment, Title VI, the Equal Protection Act of 1974, and the No Child Left Behind Act.

- The courts respect a variety of approaches to teaching students with limited English proficiency as long as it is done in good faith and produces reasonable results.

Students with Disabilities

- Federal and state laws ensure equal educational rights for disabled students; the best known of these are the IDEA, Section 504 of the Rehabilitation Act, and the Americans with Disabilities Act (ADA).

- The IDEA requires that disabled students receive free, appropriate, public education in the least restrictive environment.

- An IEP team creates an educational program for each child with disabilities, subject to the parents' approval.

- Schools must provide related services and administer medications prescribed by the student's physician and provided by the parents.

- Disabled students may be disciplined in the same manner as other students if there is no causal connection between their misbehavior and their disability. If there is, long-term suspension or expulsion is a change in placement, which can be done only with the involvement of the IEP team and the parents.

- Disabled students who are dangerous to themselves or others can be suspended for up to 10 days, (or up to 45 days in cases of weapons or drugs) during which period a different placement can be negotiated with the parents or guardians, or, if they resist, with the help of a court.

- Disabled students can also be required to take standardized tests or "high-stakes" tests, as long as they have been given adequate notice, the appropriate curriculum, and appropriate accommodations for taking such tests.

Notes

1. 163 U.S. 537 (1896).
2. 374 U.S. 483 (1954).
3. 349 U.S. 294 (1955).
4. *Grenn v. County Sch. Bd. of New Kent County*, 391 U.S. 430 (1968).
5. *Pasadena City Bd. of Educ. v. Spangler*, 427 U.S. 424 (1976).
6. *Bd. of Educ. v. Dowell*, 498 U.S. 237 (1991).
7. *Freeman v. Pitts*, 503 U.S. 467 (1992).
8. *McDonnell Douglas Corp. v. Green*, 411 U.S. 792 (1973).
9. *Pregnancy Discrimination Act*, 42 U.S.C. §2000e (K) (2003).
10. *Cleveland Bd. of Educ. v. LaFleur*, 414 U.S. 632 (1974).
11. 34 C.F.R. §106.41 (a), (b).
12. *Lantz v. Ambach*, 620 F. Supp. 663 (S.D. N.Y. 1985).
13. *Leffel v. Wis. Interscholastic Athletic Ass'n.*, 444 F. Supp. 111T (E.D. Wis. 1978).
14. There have also been numerous cases challenging policies denying gender integration of noncontact sports where schools had teams for only one gender. Title IX explicitly favors girls who want to participate on integrated teams in noncontact sports, since athletic competition for girls has historically been more limited than for boys.
15. Diana Jean Schemo, "Change in Federal Rules Backs Single-Sex Public Education," *The New York Times*, Oct. 25, 2006, p. 1.
16. *Vorchheimer v. Sch. Dist.*, 532 F.2d 880 (3rd Cir. 1976), *aff'd by an equally divided court*, 430 U.S. 703 (1977).

17. *Garrett v. Bd. of Educ.,* 775 F. Supp. 1004 (E.D. Mich. 1991).
18. *Gebser v. Lago Vista Independent Sch. Dist.,* 524 U.S. 274 (1998).
19. *Davis v. Monroe Cty. Bd. of Educ.,* 526 U.S. 629 (1999).
20. 29 U.S.C. § 621 *et seq.* (2003).
21. *Lau v. Nichols,* 414 U.S. 563 (1974).
22. *Teresa P. v. Berkeley Unified Sch. Dist.,* 724 (F. Supp. 698 (N.D. Cal. 1989).
23. *Cal. Teachers' Ass'n. v. State Bd. of Educ.,* 271 F.3d 1141 (9th Cir. 2001).
24. 20 U.S.C. § 1401 (3)(A) (2003).
25. *Bd. of Educ. v. Rowley,* 458 U.S. 176 (1982).
26. 34 C.F.R. § 300.551(b) (2003).
27. 20 U.S.C. § 1401(17) (1982).
28. *Irving Indep. Sch. Dist. v. Tatro,* 468 U.S 883 (1994).
29. *Bevin v. Wright,* 666 F. Supp. 71 (W.D. Pa. 1987).
30. *DeBord v. Bd. of Educ.,* 126 F. 3d 1102 (8th Cir. 1997).
31. *Sherry v. N.Y. State Educ. Dept.,* 479 F. Supp. 1328 (W.D. N.Y. 1979); *Keelin v. Grubbs,* 682 F.2d 595 (6th Cir. 1982).
32. 484 U.S. 305 (1988).
33. *Chapman v. Cal. Dept. of Educ.,* 279 F. Supp. 2d 981 (N.D. Cal. 2002).

chapter 9

A Teacher's Personal Life

Many teachers believe that their personal behavior away from school is their own business and should be protected by their right to privacy. Yet many administrators believe that educators teach by example, and thus should be adult role models for their students, conforming to the moral standards of the community. This chapter examines how courts have resolved this conflict between teacher freedom and administrative control. Since decisions are often determined by state statutes and district policies that reflect changing norms, the law on this topic sometimes varies among the states.

Immoral and Unprofessional Conduct

Does "Immoral" Behavior Justify Teacher Dismissal?

In 1959, Marc Morrison engaged in a brief homosexual relationship with another teacher. When the relationship was reported to Morrison's superintendent, his teaching credential was revoked for "immoral" and "unprofessional" conduct. Morrison challenged this action, and the California Supreme Court ruled in his favor. The court explained that it was dangerous to allow the terms *immoral* and *unprofessional* to be interpreted broadly; unless they could be defined narrowly, such terms could be applied to most teachers in the state. According to the court, when teachers' jobs are not affected, their private behavior is their own business and should not be a basis for discipline.[1]

Before *Morrison,* the fact that a teacher engaged in conduct a community considered immoral would have been enough to justify a teacher's dismissal. After *Morrison,* other courts began to rule that teachers could not be dismissed simply because of such out-of-school behavior unless there was evidence of a "nexus," or connection, between the conduct and the teacher's effectiveness. To determine whether a nexus exists, many judges consider factors such as the likelihood that the conduct will negatively affect students or teachers, the proximity or remoteness of the behavior, the teacher's motivation, extenuating or aggravating circumstances, and the likelihood of the conduct being repeated.

Are There Ways to Limit the Ambiguity of the Term *Immorality*?

Yes. To avoid ambiguity, laws can define and limit the term. In Wisconsin, for example, the law allows a teacher's license to be revoked for such conduct only "if there is clear and convincing evidence that the person engaged in immoral conduct, and there is a nexus between the immoral conduct and the health, welfare, safety, or education of any pupil."[2]

Is Discrimination against Homosexuals Illegal?

It is in many states and cities that prohibit discrimination based on sexual orientation. In addition, the trend in federal decisions is to rule that such discrimination violates the equal protection clause of the Fourteenth Amendment. Thus, a federal court ruled against an Ohio district that failed to renew a teacher's contract because of his sexual orientation. According to the judge, homosexuals "are entitled to at least the same protection as any other identifiable group," and hostility against homosexuals "can never be a legitimate government purpose."[3] The teacher was reinstated and compensated for loss of salary, mental anguish, and attorney's fees.

Can Teachers Be Dismissed for Being Unwed Mothers?

Probably not. In Illinois, a federal court ruled against a school that fired a teacher for being unmarried and pregnant and for deciding to raise her child as a single parent. According to the judge, "it is beyond question that [the teacher] had a substantive due process right to conceive and raise her child out of wedlock without unwarranted . . . School Board intrusion."[4]

Can Teachers Be Dismissed for Immoral or Unprofessional Conduct with Students?

Yes. Most courts do not allow teachers to be dismissed for immorality for consensual activities with adults as long as those activities do not have a negative effect on their teaching. However, judges are usually strict about immoral behavior with students, especially in the area of sexual relations. Thus, a New York court upheld the dismissal of a teacher for refusing to stop living with a 16-year-old student despite his mother's strong objections. Similarly, a Maine teacher was fired for having sexual relations with a 15-year-old neighbor, even though he had never been her student. According to the court, her poor judgment showed she was "unfit to teach," and her conduct undermined her ability to be effective in the school's program dealing with "sexual abuse and exploitation of children."[5]

In addition, courts have ruled that teachers can be dismissed for sexual conduct with students that occurred years earlier. Thus, in upholding the firing of an Alaska teacher who had a sexual relationship with a student 12 years earlier, the judge wrote that such conduct could never be "too remote" to support a teacher's dismissal.[6] Teachers, of course, can also be fired for making sexual advances toward students.

Can Teachers Be Dismissed for Sexual Relationships with Students Even after Graduation?

A recent case says they can. In that 2004 decision, a court ruled that a teacher could be denied tenure for a sexual relationship with a student nine months after she graduated. In order to prevent such relationships before graduation, wrote the court, a school board has the discretion to "act prophylactically" by "prohibiting sexual relationships between teachers and former students within a year or two of graduation."[7]

Can a Teacher Be Fired for Using Profanity or Abusive Language Toward Students?

Yes. In Colorado, a band director was dismissed for telling a troublesome student he was an "S. O. B.," and a "fucking asshole."[8] And a Pennsylvania teacher was fired for calling a student a "slut." In upholding the dismissal, a judge explained that administrators must be able to protect students from such "totally inappropriate" and abusive language by teachers.[9]

Can Teachers Be Dismissed Because of Rumors of Immoral Conduct?

No. If teachers are terminated for immoral conduct, such action should be based on facts, not rumors. This was the ruling of a Texas court in a case involving a former student who alleged that he had had sexual relations with two teachers. Although the teachers denied the allegations, which were not proven, the teachers were still dismissed. According to the administration, the widespread rumors of the allegations diminished the teachers' effectiveness "regardless of their truth or falsity." However, to allow teachers to be terminated based on allegations, wrote the court, "would create a dangerous precedent which would leave teachers particularly vulnerable to fabricated accusations by disgruntled students or parents."[10]

Are There Other Reasons Teachers Have Been Dismissed for Immoral or Unprofessional Conduct?

Yes. Here are a few cases where courts have upheld teacher termination:

- A California teacher was dismissed after she was arrested for openly engaging in sexual activity with three men at a swingers' club.
- A New York teacher was terminated after his active membership in the North American Man/Boy Love Association became public and caused severe disruption at his school.
- An Ohio coach was fired for telling a student to lie about his weight during a wrestling tournament.
- A Missouri teacher was dismissed for permitting male students to sexually harass a female student.

· ●

125

Furthermore, schools can fire teachers without first warning them if their behavior is outrageous or a clear violation of professional ethics. Examples include a counselor who disclosed an incest victim's confidences in a social setting with teachers who had no need for the information, and two teachers who allowed students to participate in a pot-smoking party at their home.

Will Courts Reverse Penalties against Teachers That Seem Harsh?

Not usually. Although courts often overturn school board decisions that violate due process, they are reluctant to reverse a board penalty because it seems harsh. In Alabama, for example, a court upheld the dismissal of a dedicated, tenured teacher for possession of firearms on school grounds after he fired his licensed pistol into the ground to scare nonstudents who attacked him at night school. Although the judges were troubled by the dismissal of this teacher, they felt required to support the board because the teacher violated school policy.[11]

Criminal Conduct

Does Conviction for a Misdemeanor Justify Dismissal?

Not necessarily. However, it may if the misdemeanor constitutes a crime of immoral or unprofessional conduct. For example, a Minnesota teacher of business ethics was fired after being convicted of theft from a company he ran with two other teachers. Similarly, a Pennsylvania court upheld the dismissal of a teacher for shoplifting because it offended community morals and was a bad example for students.

Is Conviction for a Felony Grounds for Dismissal?

Usually it is. Thus, a Delaware court upheld the dismissal of an outstanding teacher who pled guilty to a widely publicized felony of aggravated assault. According to some courts, however, conviction of a crime is not always sufficient to permanently bar a person from teaching. For example, a California court wrote that a teacher who committed a crime "paid the penalty and now seeks to discourage his students from committing similar acts" may be a more effective supporter of the law than someone who never violated it.[12]

Can Teachers Be Fired If There Is No Evidence Linking Their Crime to Their Job?

Yes, in some states. Although there was no evidence that a teacher's burglary impaired his teaching, a Kansas court upheld his dismissal because of the presumed relationship between the felonious conduct and fitness to teach. The court noted that, because of the seriousness of a felony conviction, such a conviction is also grounds to revoke a license to practice law or medicine.[13]

Can a Teacher Be Dismissed Because of Criminal Charges?

Not simply because of the charges. However, if the alleged crime relates to their job as teacher (e.g., stealing school funds, molesting students, or selling drugs), then the teacher could be suspended until the outcome of the criminal process.

If a Teacher Is Found Not Guilty of a Crime, Can He or She Still Be Fired for the Behavior That Led to That Charge?

Yes. Acquittal of a criminal charge, such as selling drugs to students, does not prevent a school from dismissing a teacher on those grounds and would not constitute double jeopardy. To convict someone of a crime, the state must prove that the person is guilty "beyond a reasonable doubt." But, to dismiss a teacher, a school only needs to show "by a preponderance of the evidence" that the teacher engaged in immoral or criminal conduct that impaired his or her teaching. This cannot be based merely on the fact of the teacher's arrest, but must be based on independent evidence.

Can a Teacher Be Dismissed Because of the Use or Possession of Illegal Drugs?

It might depend on the drug, the amount, and the circumstances. Courts, for example, might not support firing a teacher solely because the teacher was once indicted for possessing a small amount of marijuana or for growing one marijuana plant. But, judges probably would support a dismissal based on a widely publicized conviction of drug possession combined with evidence that the criminal behavior would undermine the teacher's effectiveness.

Does Mental Illness Excuse a Teacher's Criminal Behavior?

Not necessarily. Mental illness might result in a teacher being acquitted of criminal intent, but it might not protect his or job. Thus, even though a teacher's shoplifting might be caused by a mental illness, the teacher probably could still be fired if the criminal behavior destroyed his or her role model status.

Lifestyle, Citizenship, and Disability

Can a Teacher Be Prohibited from Breastfeeding Her Child in School?

It depends on the circumstances. In Florida, for example, a court ruled in favor of a teacher who was ordered to stop breastfeeding her child during her duty-free period because of a rule prohibiting teachers from bringing their children to work. According to the court, the Constitution prohibits the state from interfering with a person's "personal privacy" or "fundamental, personal liberties," which include breastfeeding.[14] While schools can restrict this liberty to prevent disruption or ensure that teachers perform their duties, schools can only interfere with this right when necessary.

Can Teachers Be Fired Because of Obesity?

Probably not solely because of obesity. In California, a seriously overweight physical education teacher was not rehired because she was unable "to serve as a model of health" and was unable to perform some aspects of the PE program, such as trampoline and gymnastics. But, since the teacher had been a successful coach and instructor, the judge stated, "Any requirement that the teachers embody all the qualities which they hope to instill in their students will be utterly impossible of fulfillment."[15] Furthermore, evidence indicated that PE teachers "need not excel at demonstration" to be competent instructors. Since there was no evidence that the teacher's weight had a negative effect on her teaching, the court ruled in her favor.

Can Teachers Be Denied Certification Because They Are Not Citizens?

Yes. Although teachers in some districts are not citizens, the U.S. Supreme Court has ruled that a state may require that public school teachers be citizens or applicants for citizenship. According to the Court, this requirement is reasonable because all teachers are role models and may influence student attitudes toward government and the role of American citizens.[16]

Can Teachers Be Required to Reside in Their School District?

According to most courts, there is a rational basis for such requirements, since teachers who live in the district are less likely to engage in illegal strikes and more likely to be involved in school and community activities and to understand the racial, social, and economic problems of their students.

Does the Family Medical Leave Act (FMLA) Apply to Teachers?

Yes. The FMLA guarantees teachers who have been employed at least one year 12 weeks of unpaid leave during any 12-month period because of the birth or adoption of a child, to care for a seriously ill child, spouse, or parent, or because of a serious health condition that makes the individual unable to teach.

Can a Teacher Be Barred from Teaching Because of AIDS?

Probably not. Although some parents want to exclude anyone with AIDS from the classroom, Section 504 of the Rehabilitation Act ensures that otherwise qualified handicapped people cannot be denied jobs because of the prejudice or ignorance of others. Therefore, when there is no risk of transmitting AIDS in the normal school setting, individuals cannot be barred from teaching just because they have been diagnosed with AIDS.

Guidelines

- Usually teachers cannot be dismissed for private consensual conduct with another adult simply because some administrators or school board members consider the conduct immoral.
- To dismiss teachers for immoral behavior, most courts require evidence that the behavior will have a negative effect on their teaching.
- To determine whether there is a nexus, or relationship, between immoral behavior and teacher effectiveness, courts might consider the notoriety of the behavior; the reactions of students, parents, and other teachers; where and when the conduct took place; and the teacher's motivation.
- Teachers may be suspended because of a criminal indictment if their alleged crime relates to their job.
- Teachers may be fired if convicted of a serious and notorious crime even without evidence that it is related to their teaching effectiveness.

- Courts usually uphold the dismissals of teachers involved in immoral conduct with students without requiring evidence of its effect on their teaching. This is especially true regarding sexual advances or sexual relationships between teachers and students, even if consensual and even if they occurred years earlier.

- Districts may refuse to hire teachers if they are not citizens or refuse to live in the district.

- Schools may not refuse to hire or discriminate against teachers solely because of their disability.

- The law concerning dismissal of teachers for immoral, unprofessional, or illegal conduct varies depending on the state or district and the circumstances of the case.

Notes

1. *Morrison v. State Bd. of Educ.*, 461 P.2d 375 (Cal. 1968).
2. Wis. Admin. Code § PI 3.04 (1989).
3. *Glover v. Williamsburg Local Sch. Dist. Bd. of Educ.*, 20 F. Supp. 2d 1160 (S.D. Ohio 1998).
4. *Eckmann v. Bd. of Educ. of Hawthorn Sch. Dist.*, 636 F. Supp. 1214 (N.D. Ill. 1986).
5. *Elvin v. City of Waterville*, 573 A.2d 381 (Me. 1990).
6. *Toney v. Fairbanks North Star Borough Sch. Dist.*, 881 P.2d 1112 (Alaska 1994).
7. *Flaskamp v. Dearborn Public Schools*, 385 F.3d 935 (6th Cir. 2004).
8. *Ware v. Morgan County Sch. Dist.*, 748 P.2d 1295 (Colo. 1988).
9. *Bovino v. Bd. of Sch. Directors of Indiana Area Sch. Dist.*, 377 A.2d 1284 (Pa. 1977).
10. *Peaster Indep. Sch. Dist. v. Glodfelty*, 63 S. W.3d 1 (Tex. App.—Fort Worth 2001).
11. *Burton v. Ala. State Tenure Comm.*, 601 So.2d 113 (Ala. Civ. App. 1992).
12. *Bd. of Educ. of Long Beach v. Jack M.*, 139 Cal. Rptr. 700 (Cal. 1977).
13. *Hainline v. Bond*, 824 P.2d 758 (Kan. 1992).
14. *Dike v. Sch. Bd. of Orange Cnty., Florida*, 650 F.2d 783 (5th Cir. 1981).
15. *Blodgett v. Bd. of T'ees, Tamalpais Union High Sch. Dist.*, 97 Cal. Rptr. 406 (Cal. Ct. App. 1971).
16. *Ambach v. Norwick*, 441 U.S. 68 (1979).

chapter 10

Parents' Rights in Educating Their Children and Controlling Their School Records

Parents have a variety of rights and choices in educating their children in public or private schools or at home. They also have the right to review their children's educational records and prevent access to outsiders. This chapter outlines these rights and choices.

Parental Choice

What Choices Do Parents Have in Educating Their Children?

In *Pierce v. Society of Sisters*,[1] the Supreme Court recognized the basic right of parents and guardians "to direct the upbringing and education of children under their control." Among other things, the Court said, "The child is not the mere creature of the state; those who nurture him and direct his destiny have the right, coupled with the high duty, to recognize and prepare him for additional obligations."

Since our Constitution does not mention education, schooling is basically a function of state governments. Most states, however, delegate much power over schooling to local school boards who function within state guidelines, the Constitution, and federal laws.

Consistent with the *Pierce* case, courts have held that the state's requirement that children attend school can be met through public or private schools, secular or religious. After the publication of *A Nation at Risk* in 1983, warning that public schools were creating a "rising tide of mediocrity that threatens our very future as a nation and a people," various reforms arose to improve schools. First among these were charter schools.

What Are Charter Schools?

Charter schools are semiautonomous public schools created by a contract or charter between the school's organizers and a sponsor—either a state department of education or a school district. The creators of the schools are held accountable for achieving the educational goals and, in turn, the school is exempt from many restrictions that apply to traditional public schools. Initially, the federal government provided funds to support charter schools through several statutes.[2] As of June 2005, 41 states, plus Puerto Rico and Washington, D.C., have charter school laws and 37 operate public charter schools. The largest number of charter schools are in California, Arizona, Florida, Texas, and Michigan.[3] Since there is great variability in the quality of charter schools, it is up to parents to investigate and assess the schools that might be available in their community.

Do Voucher Plans Enhance Parental Choice?

Yes. In recent years, a few states have provided public funds to parents for "vouchers" or "certificates," which are endorsed to the private school where their children are enrolled. The value of the vouchers depends on the particular program and is usually related to the state aid per student during the particular school year. Vouchers in Milwaukee, Wisconsin, and Cleveland, Ohio, can be used in religious or secular schools as long as students are not required to participate in religious activities. Some states, such as Maine, prohibit the use of vouchers in religious schools.

May Parents Choose Homeschooling for Their Children?

Yes, they may, if they satisfy the conditions specified by their particular state. Today, approximately 2 million children are homeschooled in the United States, and their number is increasing yearly. Most parents choose to homeschool their children for religious reasons. States usually require that the alternative education be equivalent to public schooling and that systematic reporting be made to the local school superintendent to enable the state to supervise the alternative schooling.

Some states' courts are quite liberal in their interpretation of their state's statutes, while others are quite strict. For example, in a case that arose in Maine in 1983, the court held that the state has the power to impose reasonable regulations for the control and duration of basic education.[4] When parents refused to submit their plans for homeschooling to school authorities for approval, they were fined on the grounds that their children were habitually truant. Similarly, a Kansas court found that home instruction that was unplanned and unscheduled, by a mother who was not certified or accredited, did not satisfy the state compulsory attendance law.[5] And a California court held that children enrolled in a correspondence course were not receiving equivalent instruction.[6] California is one of the few states that require that the person conducting the home schooling be certified to teach.

Must State Laws Be Clear and Unambiguous?

Yes. Thus, the Georgia Supreme Court held that if the law does not provide clear guidance to a person of ordinary intelligence, then it is unconstitutionally vague.[7] As a result of such holdings, many states have revised their homeschooling laws in recent years to make them more clear and specific.

Most of the cases challenging homeschooling laws have been brought by parents who claim to be educating their children at home for religious reasons. Courts in different states have reached different conclusions in these cases. Since the U.S. Supreme Court has never ruled directly on this issue, one must examine the case law of the particular state where the conflict arises.

Can Handicapped Children Be Homeschooled?

Yes, if the standards of the state are satisfied. Vermont, for example, has a home study law that requires a "minimum course of study . . . adapted in each area of study . . . to the age and ability of each child and adapted to the handicapping condition of the child."[8]

Do Homeschoolers Have a Right to Participate in School Sports?

No. In a case that arose in New York, a 14-year-old homeschooled girl asked to participate in the interscholastic sports program of the district of her residence. A state board of education rejected her request for it specified that only students in regular attendance could participate in interscholastic sports. She went to court, claiming her due process and equal protection rights were violated. She lost on both grounds.

The court held that she had no property right to participate in the sports program that would be protected by the due process clause. The court said the regulation did not violate the equal protection clause since it was reasonably related to a legitimate state purpose.[9] A Michigan court reached the same conclusion in 2004.[10] Although most courts have ruled the same way, there have been exceptions. For instance, in Arkansas and New Hampshire, courts have found a property interest in participating in extracurricular activities.[11]

Since most cases addressing a federal constitutional right to participate in extracurricular activities denied such a right, efforts have been directed at state legislatures to enact laws specifically permitting participation. Several states, including Iowa, Oregon, and Washington, have enacted such laws. School districts and interscholastic athletic associations tend to oppose such laws, claiming that they place undue hardships on the administration of public schools.

In sum, whether a particular homeschooling teaching arrangement satisfies the law depends on the constitution and statutes of the particular state as well as the courts' interpretation of those laws. It also depends on the parents' qualifications to teach, whether systematic instruction is provided, how well the children are progressing in comparison with their age mates in public schools, and the adequacy of a reporting system supervised by a responsible school official.

Do Homeschoolers Have a Right to Part-Time Enrollment in Public Schools?

No, they do not if there is a school board policy requiring full-time attendance, ruled the Tenth Circuit Court in an Oklahoma case.[12] (The school board created this policy because the state of Oklahoma reimbursed school districts only for students enrolled full-time.) State laws vary on this issue and must be examined in each state, along with the policy of the district where the issue arises.

Can Parents Object to Certain Courses or Materials?

That depends on the grounds of their objections. The most common bases for objections are religious. The best known is parental objection to the inclusion of evolution in the curriculum. When the Arkansas legislature forbade the teaching of evolution in public schools, the Supreme Court declared the state law unconstitutional as a violation of the establishment clause of the First Amendment.[13] Efforts to include "creationism" or "intelligent design" in the curriculum have also been struck down on the same ground.[14]

A highly controversial case arose in Tennessee in 1987 when parents objected to the use of the Holt, Rinehart, and Winston reading series, claiming that stories in the series taught values offensive to their religion.[15] A majority of the judges ruled against the parents, and concluded that accommodation of every parent's religious claim "will leave public education in shreds." Thus, as long as students are not required to affirm or deny religious beliefs, courts are likely to protect schools' discretion in the use of curricular materials.

Parental Control of Student Records

In 1974, Congress passed the Family Educational Rights and Privacy Act, also knows as FERPA or the Buckley Amendment, to define who may and may not see student records.

Why Did Congress Pass the Family Educational Rights and Privacy Act?

Congress acted because of abuses in the use of student records, especially the tendency of schools to provide access to the records to outsiders but to deny access to students' parents.

What Are the Main Features of FERPA?

The act contains five important features:

1. It requires school districts to inform parents of their rights under the act each year.
2. It guarantees parents the right to inspect and review the educational records of their children.
3. It establishes procedures through which parents can challenge the accuracy of student records.

4. It protects the confidentiality of student records by preventing disclosure of personally identifiable information to outsiders without prior parental consent.

5. It entitles parents to file complaints with the U.S. Department of Education concerning alleged failures to comply with the act.

The act, which has been amended many times, applies to all public and private schools and educational agencies receiving federal education funds, either directly or indirectly.[16] Parents or guardians may assert their children's rights of access and consent until they become 18 years old or begin attending a postsecondary institution; after this, these rights will only be accorded to the student.

Right of Access

What Education Records Are Accessible under the Act?

Education records include any information maintained by a school (or a person acting for a school) that is directly related to a current student regardless of whether the record is handwritten, print, tape, film, microfilm, or electronic form. The information may be in a teacher's or principal's desk as well as in an official student file.

How Does the Act Guarantee Parental Access?

FERPA states that no federal funds will be made available to any school that prevents parents from exercising "the right to inspect and review the education records of their children." This includes the right (1) to be informed about the kinds and location of education records maintained by the school and the officials responsible for them, and (2) to receive an explanation or interpretation of the records if requested. Officials must comply with a parental request to inspect records "within a reasonable time, but in no case more than 45 days after the request." Either parent (including a noncustodial parent) has the right to inspect the records, unless prohibited by court order.

Do Parents Have the Right to See Teachers' Personal Notes about Their Children?

No. FERPA does not give parents the right to review the personal notes of teachers, counselors, and administrators if these records are used *only* as a "personal memory aid," are in their "sole possession," and are not revealed to any other individual except a substitute teacher.

What Other Records Are Not Accessible?

Parents do not have the right to see records of a physician, psychologist, or other recognized professional used *only* in connection with their child's treatment. Parents also have no right to see records of a law enforcement unit of the school maintained *solely* for police purposes, or job-related records of students who are employees of the school.

Can Students Waive Their Right of Access?

Yes. Individuals who are applicants for admission to postsecondary institutions may waive their right to inspect confidential letters of recommendation. Although institutions may not require such waivers "as a condition of admission," they may "request" them. These waivers must be signed by the individual students, regardless of age, rather than by their parents.

How Does FERPA Restrict Access to Outsiders?

The act requires that a school obtain "the written consent of the parent . . . before disclosing personally identifiable information from the education records of a student." The consent must be signed and include the specific records to be disclosed, the purpose, and to whom the disclosure may be made.

Do Noncustodial Parents Have Access to Their Children's Records?

Yes. A parent's right to inspect and review the educational records of their children applies equally to noncustodial parents who do not live with their children unless their access has been prohibited by a court order or other legal document. In ruling that a custodial parent could not prohibit a noncustodial parent from having access to his son's records under FERPA, a judge wrote that schools should make educational information "available to both parents of every child fortunate enough to have two parents interested in his welfare."[17]

May Noncustodial Parents Visit Their Children in School?

FERPA does not address this issue. The answer usually depends on district policy. In Medford, Massachusetts, for example, both custodial and noncustodial parents have the right to visit their children briefly in school and to participate in parent–teacher conferences. However, the noncustodial parent cannot remove the children from school without the agreement of the custodial parent.[18]

Are There Exceptions to the Consent Requirement?

Yes, there are several. For example, prior consent is not required when education records are shared (1) with teachers and "other school officials" in the district who have "legitimate educational interests," (2) with officials of another school in which the student seeks to enroll (provided the parents are notified), (3) with persons for whom the information is necessary "to protect the health or safety of the student or other individuals," (4) pursuant to a subpoena issued by a court, and (5) in connection with financial aid for which a student has applied.

Does FERPA Prohibit a School from Releasing a Teacher's College Transcript without the Teacher's Consent?

No. In Texas, a parent, concerned about the quality of public education requested access to the academic records of a teacher under the state's Open Records Act. The teacher claimed that the disclosure would violate her privacy rights under FERPA. But a federal court ruled that FERPA was intended to protect only student records, not the records of a school employee.[19] However, a teacher's personnel file may be protected from public disclosure under the laws of some states.

Does FERPA Require Schools to Restrict Distribution of Personal Student Information in School Newspapers?

It depends on the sources of the information. If the information in the newspaper came from student records, printing it would violate FERPA. But the act does not protect information derived from a source (such as other students) independent of school records.

What Information about Students Can Be Shared without Consent?

A school has discretion to disclose "directory information" from the education records of a student without requiring prior parental consent. *Directory information* includes such facts as a student's name, address, e-mail address, phone number, date and place of birth, field of study, sports activities, dates of attendance, awards received, photograph, and similar information. Before freely releasing such information, a school must try to notify parents of current students about what facts it regards as directory information and of the parents' right to refuse to permit the release of such information. It is the parents' obligation to notify the school in writing if they refuse. A school may release directory information about *former* students without first trying to notify them.

Does FERPA Prohibit the Release of School Reports about Altercations between Teachers and Students?

It did not in a 2004 Ohio case, when a parent sought school records involving assaults by a teacher. The school district argued that the records were protected by FERPA since they included the names of students. But a federal court ruled that the information sought by the parent was not protected by FERPA because it covered "records directly related to teachers and only tangentially related to students." Moreover, the case did not involve systematic invasion of student privacy which FERPA prohibits, but the permissible disclosure of a narrowly defined discovery request "pursuant to a court order on a case-by-case basis."[20]

Can Teachers Be Disciplined for Disclosing Confidential Information about Students?

Yes, whether the information is protected by FERPA or not. Although FERPA does not cover disclosure of confidential information that is not recorded, the sharing of such information by a teacher with persons who have no need to know is usually unprofessional and unethical and may violate state privacy laws. Thus, such a disclosure would be a valid reason for disciplinary action. On the other hand, FERPA cannot be used as a defense by teachers or counselors for failure to report reasonable concerns about students who are abused, neglected, or are suicidal.

Does FERPA Prevent Administrators from Sharing Critical Information about Students with Teachers?

No. The amendment does not prohibit administrators from sharing information with teachers or with anyone for whom the information is necessary to protect the health and safety of students or teachers. In addition, FERPA was amended in 1994 to explicitly allow schools to share with any teacher or school official who has a legitimate interest in the student's behavior information about disciplinary action taken against the student for conduct "that posed a significant risk to the safety or well-being" of a member of the school community.[21]

Can Schools Destroy Student Records?

Yes. If state law does not determine how long student records must be kept, schools may destroy some or all of a student's educational record at any time, except when there is an outstanding request to see them and except as provided under IDEA for special education students.

Must Parents Be Informed of Their Rights under the Buckley Amendment?

Yes. Every school must give the parents of all current students "annual notice" of their rights under the act. Schools must indicate where parents can obtain copies of the school's policy for implementing and protecting these rights, and must inform them of their "right to file complaints" for the school's failure to comply with the act.

Do Parents Have a Right to Challenge Their Children's Records?

Yes. If the parents of a student believe that a school record is "inaccurate or misleading or violates the privacy or other rights of the student," they may request that the school amend it. If the school refuses, it must advise the parents of their rights to a hearing. The hearing may be conducted by anyone who does not have a direct interest in its outcome. Parents must be given "a full and fair opportunity" to present their evidence and may be represented by counsel, at their own expense. Hearing officers must make their decision in writing "based solely on the evidence presented at the hearing," and it must include the reasons and evidence to support their decision. The decision is final and there is no appeal.

If, as a result of the hearing, the hearing officers decide the record was inaccurate or misleading, the school must amend the record accordingly. But if the officers decide that the information was correct, the school must inform the parents of "the right to place in the education records of the student a statement commenting upon the information . . . and/or setting forth any reasons for disagreeing with the decision" of the school. Such explanation must be maintained by the school as part of the student's record; if the contested portion of the record is disclosed to anyone, the parents' explanation must also be disclosed.

May Parents or Students Contest the Appropriateness of a Grade?

No. A federal appeals court held that FERPA does not give judges authority to rule on disputes about the wisdom of a teacher's grades. As the court explained, FERPA gave parents the right to challenge a misleading or improperly recorded grade, but they "could not . . . contest whether the teacher should have assigned a higher grade."[22]

Does FERPA Prohibit Students from Grading Each Other's Classroom Work or Assignments?

No, ruled the U.S. Supreme Court in *Owasso v. Falvo.*[23] This 2002 case began in Tulsa, Oklahoma, when Mrs. Falvo objected to the practice of her children's teacher who had students exchange papers, grade them, and return them to the students who prepared them. The teacher then asked the students to call out the scores which she entered in a grade book. Mrs. Falvo asked the school to prohibit peer grading, which embarrassed her children, but the Supreme Court did not agree.

If homework or class work were considered education records protected by FERPA, wrote the Court, "this would impose substantial burdens on the teachers across the country," since it would force instructors to correct daily student assignments and "would make it much more difficult for teachers to give students immediate guidance." The Court concluded that the grades on student papers are not covered under FERPA "at least until the teacher has collected them and recorded them in his or her grade book."

Are Special Education Students Entitled to Additional Rights?

Yes. In addition to their rights under FERPA, special education students have additional rights under the Individuals with Disabilities Education Act (IDEA). For example, schools are required to maintain IEPs and evaluations for at least three years to document compliance with IDEA. In addition, IDEA requires schools to provide parents with access to student records before any IEP meeting or special education hearing.

Are There Any Procedures to Enforce FERPA?

Yes. There are detailed federal regulations concerning enforcement. The Family Policy Compliance Office of the U.S. Department of Education has been established to "investigate, process, and review violations and complaints." After receiving written complaints regarding alleged violations, the office will notify the school and provide an opportunity to respond. After its investigation, the office will send its findings to the complainant and the school. If there has been a violation, the office will indicate the specific steps the school must take to be in compliance. If the school does not comply, a review board hearing will be held. If the review board determines "that compliance cannot be secured by voluntary means," federal education funds will be terminated.

Thousands of complaints have been received by the Family Policy Compliance Office, and about 80 percent of them have been resolved informally through phone calls to the school districts. As of August 2005, there have been over 1,000 formal investigations.[24] No cases have yet been referred to the review board; thus, federal funds have never been terminated for noncompliance.

In addition to enforcing FERPA, the Family Policy Compliance Office tries to help educators understand the act. Its staff will consult with teachers and administrators by letter or phone and will answer questions concerning the act, its regulations, and their interpretation and application in specific school districts.[25]

Can Parents Sue Schools for Violating Their FERPA Rights?

No. FERPA does not give individuals the right to sue a school district for violations. The act is only enforceable by the federal Department of Education, which can withhold funds from schools that have "a policy or practice" of releasing educational records in violation of FERPA.

Guidelines

Parental Choice

- While state laws may require all children between certain ages to attend school, children may attend public or private schools, religious or secular, or they may be homeschooled.

- Charter schools are free from many of the restrictions that apply to public schools, but charter schools are then accountable for achieving their educational goals.

- Voucher programs enhance parental choice by providing some public funds that can be used in private schools, religious or secular, unless the laws of the particular state forbid the use of public funds in religious schools.

- Parents may homeschool their children if they satisfy their state's laws for homeschooling, which usually require the approval of homeschooling plans by the local public school authorities.

- Handicapped children may also be homeschooled provided that parents follow state regulations.

- In general, homeschooled children have no right to participate in extracurricular activities or school sports, or to enroll part-time unless the school district allows it.

- If parents have religious objections to some parts of the curriculum (such as sex education), many schools will excuse their children from participation.

Parental Control of Student Records

- The Family Educational Rights and Privacy Act guarantees parents (including noncustodial parents) the right to review the educational records of their children.

- FERPA prohibits disclosure of student records to outsiders without a parent's written consent.

- Parental consent is not required when records are shared with teachers and other school officials or when necessary for the protection of health or safety.

- Parents are entitled to a hearing to challenge the accuracy of their children's records, but they have no right to contest the wisdom of a teacher's grade.

- If parents believe schools are not complying with FERPA, they have a right to file a complaint with the U.S. Department of Education. However, the act can only be enforced by the department, not by parents.

- FERPA requires schools to annually inform parents of their rights under the act.

- When students become 18 or attend postsecondary schools, they assume their parents' rights under the act.

Notes

1. 268 U.S. 510 (1925).
2. 20 U.S.C.S. §5888; 20 U.S.C.S. § 8061–8067.
3. Bob Hass, "Promoting Educational Innovation: A Look at Two Charter High Schools," *Stanford Educator* (Spring 2005).

4. *State v. McDonough,* 468 A.2d 977 (Me. 1983).

5. *In re Sawyer,* 672 P.2d 1093 (Kan. 1983).

6. *In re Shinn,* 16 Cal. Rptr. 165 (Cal. Ct. App. 1961).

7. *Roemhild v. State,* 308 S.E. 2d.154 (Ga. 1983).

8. *In re S. M.,* 824 A.2d 593 (Vt. 2003).

9. *Broadstreet v. Sobol,* 630 N. Y. S.2d 486 (N.Y. Sup. Ct. 1995).

10. *Reid v. Kenowa Hills Pub. Sch.,* 680 N.W.2d 62 (Mich. Ct. App. 2004).

11. *Boyd v. Bd. of Directors of McGehee Sch. Dist.,* 612 F. Supp. 86 (D. Ark. 1985); *Duffey v. H. H. Interschol. Athletic Ass'n.,* 446 A.2d 462 (N.H. 1982).

12. *Swanson v. Guthrie Indep. Sch. Dist.,* 135 F.3d 694 (10th Cir. 1998).

13. *Epperson v. State of Arkansas,* 393 U.S. 97 (1968).

14. *Selman v. Cobb County Sch. Dist.,* 2005 U.S. Dist. Ct. Lexis 432 (2005); *Kitzmiller v. Dover Area Sch. District,* 400 F. Supp. 2d 707, (M.D. Pa. 2005).

15. *Mozert v. Hawkins Co. Bd. of Educ.,* 827 F.2d 1058 (6th Cir. 1987).

16. The text of the act is in Title 20, Section 1232g of the *United States Code Annotated* (2000). Regulations for implementing the act are in the *Code of Federal Regulations* Title 34, Part 99 (2004). Quotations about the act in this chapter are from the *Code of Federal Regulations,* unless otherwise indicated.

17. *Page v. Rotterdam-Mohonasen Central Sch. Dist.,* 441 N.Y. S. 2d 323 (N.Y. Sup. Ct. 1981).

18. "Custodial and Noncustodial Parents' Rights and Responsibilities," School Committee Policy #51, Medford Public Schools (July 13, 2006).

19. *Klein Independent Sch. Dist. v. Mattox,* 830 F.2d 576 (5th Cir. 1987).

20. *Ellis v. Cleveland Municipal Sch. Dist.,* 309 F. Supp. 2d 1019 (N.D. Ohio 2004).

21. 20 U.S.C.A. § 1232g (h) (1997).

22. *Tarka v. Cunningham,* 917 F.2d 890 (5th Cir. 1990).

23. *Owasso Indep. Sch. Dist. No. 1-011 v. Falvo,* 534 U.S. 426 (2002).

24. Telephone interview with J. E. Smith, Program Specialist, Family Policy Compliance Office (August 25, 2005).

25. For copies of the regulations or a Model Policy Document for elementary and secondary schools, contact the Family Policy Compliance Office, U.S. Department of Education, 400 Maryland Avenue, SW, Washington, DC 20202, or phone (202) 260-3887.

chapter 11

The No Child Left Behind Act and Other Current Controversies

This chapter highlights controversial issues that have recently emerged or that continue to be among teachers' educational and legal concerns: The No Child Left Behind Act, high-stakes testing, teacher testing, AIDS awareness, condom distribution, protection of homosexual teachers and students, compulsory community service, and frivolous lawsuits.

The No Child Left Behind Act

The No Child Left Behind (NCLB) Act of 2001, which amended the Elementary and Secondary Education Act of 1965, represents the most significant expansion of the role of the federal government in education in more than 35 years.[1]

What Are the Main Features of NCLB?

NCLB requires each state to develop a plan that addresses academic standards, academic assessments, and accountability. The plan holds local districts accountable for student achievement and for ensuring adequate yearly progress (AYP). Districts must administer tests each year in grades 3–8 and once during high school in math and reading. Science must be tested once during grades 3–5, 6–9, and 10–12. Districts must issue annual report cards which identify schools that need improvement and that show how students scored on the statewide academic assessments, compared to other students in the state. In addition, the report cards must disaggregate student achievement by gender, race, poverty, disability, and English proficiency. The act requires that all teachers of core subjects be highly qualified and that, by 2014, all students will meet the state's proficiency level of academic achievement. Charter schools are subject to the same accountability and assessment requirements as public schools.

What Is a "Highly Qualified" Teacher or Paraprofessional?

According to NCLB, a highly qualified teacher has obtained full state certification or passed the state teacher licensing examination. For new teachers, this means they must hold a bachelor's degree and have passed a rigorous state test.

NCLB requires that paraprofessionals in districts receiving Title I funds obtain an associate's degree or demonstrate, through formal assessment, the ability to assist in teaching reading, writing, and mathematics.

What Are the Consequences If Schools Fail to Meet Adequate Yearly Progress?

Schools that fail to meet AYP for two consecutive years must be identified as "needing improvement," must be provided technical assistance, and must allow their students to participate in a public school choice plan. There are increasingly significant consequences for schools that continue to fail to meet AYP. After three years, students should receive "supplemental services"; after four years, "corrective actions," such as replacing school staff or implementing a new curriculum, are required; and, after five years, the school must be "restructured," including a state takeover or reopening as a charter school.

Can Parents Sue to Enforce NCLB?

No. The NCLB Act contains no private right of action for parents to sue to enforce the act. Instead, the sole remedy in the NCLB Act for noncompliance is through action of the U.S. Secretary of Education.

Does NCLB Include Other Requirements?

Yes, there are a variety of requirements that have little to do with academic achievement. These include requiring that districts certify that they have no policy prohibiting constitutionally protected prayer, that districts do not discriminate against Boy Scouts, that sex education include the health benefits of abstinence, that military recruiters have access to schools, that students in "persistently dangerous" schools be allowed to transfer to a safe school, and that teachers be protected against liability for disciplining students.

High-Stakes Testing

High-stakes testing has become the popular way to refer to the use of standardized tests that may lead to serious consequences. Depending on state laws and school district policies, these tests may be used for tracking students, for promotions, and for awarding diplomas. Because many schools have used "social promotion" during the recent past, the change to high-stakes testing brought on significant failures in schools and widespread public protests.

These failures and protests have led to lawsuits challenging high-stakes tests on behalf of children with disabilities, those with limited English, and racial and ethnic minorities. Laws and regulations related to high-stakes tests require appropriate accommodation for students with disabilities. For all students, the tests must be valid and reliable and assess the curriculum taught to the children. High-stakes tests that have met these criteria have been upheld by the courts.

Teacher Testing

During recent years, a movement arose to administer competency testing to candidates for certification and even for recertification. Not surprisingly, this development led to disagreements and to a variety of legal challenges. These challenges face great difficulties if the competency test used by the state is a valid measure of the job-related knowledge and skill, if there is reasonable time to prepare for the test, and if it does not discriminate on the basis of race, national origin, religion, or gender.

In 2002, for example, teachers challenged the Massachusetts Board of Education requirement that math teachers in low-performing schools take a test to evaluate their mastery of the subject prior to renewing their licenses.[2] The teachers claimed the requirement violated their due process and equal protection rights. But the state's highest court disagreed. It explained that assessing math teachers' knowledge was a reasonable way to evaluate one possible reason for poor student performance and that the requirement ensured that teacher deficiencies could be addressed through professional development prior to relicensure. If protected groups such as racial or ethnic minorities or women can show a disparate impact on their members as a consequence of the competency test, the school district must show that the selection criterion is job-related, that there is educational necessity for using it, and that there is no better alternative way to achieve its objective.

Frivolous Lawsuits

To many educators, it sometimes appears as though disgruntled students and their parents can sue schools simply because they resent a teacher's critical judgment about their child or are angry about an administrator's disciplinary decision. Even when the plaintiff's case is dismissed, educators often feel as though they were victims of legal harassment because defendants often pay a high emotional and financial price to defend against a suit although they did nothing illegal. However, victims of such suits are not always without a remedy.

Lawyers can be punished for filing frivolous lawsuits. In New Jersey, for example, a lawyer was fined $100,000 for a pattern of frivolous suits against local teachers and administrators because he repeatedly violated the *Federal Rules of Civil Procedure*.[3] Rule 11 states that, by filing a case, an attorney is certifying that the claims are warranted by law and have "evidentiary support." If this rule is violated, a judge may impose sanctions on the attorney. This is what occurred in the New Jersey case as there was no basis in law or in fact for the due process suit that was brought on behalf of a student who admitted the charges against him and received more process than was due. In another federal case, the judge criticized parents and their attorney for filing a suit to protect the alleged "rights" of students who were prohibited from marching in their graduation after becoming drunk and disorderly on a class trip. The judge thought the parents would have been "too embarrassed to go to court" over this "tempest in a teapot," and he fined the lawyer for failing to do "a few minutes of legal research" through which he "could easily have discovered" that his claims were "patently frivolous."[4]

AIDS Awareness and Condom Distribution

More than 30 states require AIDS education, and many schools provide condoms to students. Yet many parents argue that these programs violate their religious beliefs or parental rights.

In Massachusetts, for example, parents charged that an AIDS awareness assembly violated their rights to direct their children's education, created a sexually hostile environment, and required their permission. But a federal appeals court rejected these arguments. It explained that parents have no right to dictate the curriculum. Furthermore, the assembly did not violate Title IX since the offensive speech was not threatening or humiliating, was not directed at the plaintiffs' children, and was intended to educate about AIDS, not to create a hostile environment.[5]

There is judicial disagreement about whether condom distribution without parental consent might violate state law. In New York, for example, a court ruled that a state law requiring parental consent for medical treatment applied to condom distribution, which is "a health service for the prevention of disease," not an educational program.[6] In contrast, the Massachusetts Supreme Judicial Court upheld a district program that distributed free condoms from the school nurse to all students in grades 7–12 who requested them. The court explained that the program did not violate parental rights since it was not coercive or compulsory and since parents could tell their children not to participate. Therefore, the court concluded that "neither an opt-out provision nor parental notification is required by the Federal Constitution."[7]

Protection of Homosexual Students and Teachers

Whether gay and lesbian teachers and students need special legal protection and, if so, the protection they should receive continues to be a divisive issue in many communities and varies with changing state and local laws. At least 15 states prohibit sexual orientation discrimination in employment.[8] And more than 140 cities and counties prohibit such discrimination.[9] Nevertheless, a few cities and states have repealed gay rights laws.[10] However, even in states where no laws specifically protect gay and lesbian teachers, recent federal decisions have held that they cannot be discriminated against merely because of their sexual orientation.

Some states provide special protection for homosexual students and encourage support groups and teacher training about gay and lesbian issues.[11] And districts might be held liable for damages if they are deliberately indifferent to the abuse of homosexual students in their schools.

In recent years, gay/straight student alliances have been organized in public schools. Furthermore, federal courts have ruled that under the Equal Access Act, such student clubs must be able to use school facilities like all other extracurricular organizations. On the other hand, a few school boards have banned all extracurricular groups rather than recognize gay/straight organizations. Thus, despite the Equal Access Act, conflicts about gay and lesbian student organizations are likely to continue. (For more on student organizations, see Chapter 5.)

Compulsory Community Service

In recent years, increasing numbers of schools have instituted mandatory community service programs. They range from a statewide requirement in Maryland (calling for 75 hours of service before graduation) to district requirements of 40 to 270 hours over four years. Some parents have objected to these requirements as a form of unconstitutional "involuntary servitude" and a violation of parental rights without an opt-out provision. However, a federal appeals court has rejected these arguments. The court explained that the program was not a form of unconstitutional involuntary servitude because it was educational, not exploitive. Moreover, the program did not unreasonably interfere with parental rights since schools have a compelling interest in teaching the value of good citizenship and social responsibility.[12] Thus, educational, compulsory community service programs rest on solid legal foundations despite periodic legal challenges.

Guidelines

- The No Child Left Behind Act holds school districts accountable for student achievement and adequate yearly progress (AYP) through annual testing in math and reading.
- Schools that fail to meet AYP initially receive additional assistance, but after four years will require corrective action.

- High-stakes tests usually will be upheld by the courts if they assess the curriculum taught to the children.

- Teacher competency tests will be upheld if they do not discriminate and are a valid measure of job-related knowledge and skill.

- Lawyers can be fined for filing frivolous lawsuits that have no basis in law or fact.

- Schools can require AIDS education despite parental objections.

- Whether schools can provide free condom distribution without parental consent varies according to state law and district policy.

- Many states and cities prohibit employment discrimination against gay and lesbian individuals. Even without such laws, federal courts tend to prohibit discrimination merely because of sexual orientation.

- Compulsory community service programs have withstood legal challenges because they teach social responsibility.

Notes

1. NCLB, Public Law 107-110, 20 U.S.C. § 6301 (2001).
2. *Mass. Fed. of Teachers v. Bd. of Educ.*, 767 N. E.2d 549 (Mass. 2002).
3. *Giangrasso v. Kittatinny Regional High Sch. Bd. of Educ.*, 865 F. Supp. 1133 (D. N.J. 1994).
4. *Carlino v. Gloucester City High Sch.*, 57 F. Supp. 2d 1 (D. N.J. 1999).
5. *Brown v. Hot, Sexy, and Safer Productions, Inc.*, 68 F.3d 525 (1st Cir. 1995).
6. *Alfonso v. Fernandez*, 606 N.Y. S.2d 259 (N. Y. App. Div. 1993).
7. *Curtis v. Sch. Committee of Falmouth*, 652 N. E. 2d 580 (Mass. 1995).
8. Stephen Clark, "Prospectives: Federal Jurisprudence, State Autonomy: A Gay Liberationist Perspective," 66 *Albany Law Review* 719 (2003).
9. Lambda Legal Defense and Education Fund, *Summary of States, Cities, Counties Which Prohibit Discrimination Based on Sexual Orientation,* www. Lambdalegal. org/cgi-bin/iowa/news/resources.html?record=217 (visited Sept. 9, 2005).
10. *Lesbian and Gay Rights Docket,* ACLU, N.Y. (1996), pp. 5–7.
11. On December 10, 1993, Massachusetts Governor William Weld signed into law a statute banning discrimination against gays in schools. In 2001, the Massachusetts Department of Education allocated $750,000 to support safe school programs for gay and lesbian students.
12. *Immediato v. Rye Neck Sch. Dist.*, 73 F.3d 454 (2d Cir. 1996).

Selected Provisions of the U.S. Constitution

Article I

Section 8. The Congress shall have Power To lay and collect Taxes, Duties, Imposts and Excises, to pay the Debts and provide for the common Defence and general Welfare of the United States; . . .

Article III

Section 1. The judicial Power of the United States, shall be vested in one supreme Court, and in such inferior Courts as the Congress may from time to time ordain and establish. The Judges, both of the supreme and inferior Courts, shall hold their Offices during good Behaviour, and shall, at stated Times, receive for their Services a Compensation, which shall not be diminished during their Continuance in Office. . . .

Section 2. The judicial Power shall extend to all Cases, in Law and Equity, arising under this Constitution, the Laws of the United States and Treaties made, or which shall be made, under their Authority; . . . to Controversies to which the United States shall be a Party;—to Controversies between two or more States;—between a State and Citizens of another State;—between Citizens of different States;—between Citizens of the same State claiming Lands under the Grants of different States, and between a State, or the Citizens thereof, and foreign States, Citizens or Subjects. . . .

Article VI

This Constitution, and the Laws of the United States which shall be made in Pursuance thereof; and all Treaties made . . . shall be the supreme Law of the Land; and the Judges in every State shall be bound thereby, any Thing in the Constitution or Laws of any State to the Contrary notwithstanding.

Amendment I [1791]

Congress shall make no law respecting an establishment of religion, or prohibiting the free exercise thereof; or abridging the freedom of speech, or of the press; or the right of the people peaceably to assemble, and to petition the Government for a redress of grievances.

Amendment IV [1791]

The right of the people to be secure in their persons, houses, papers, and effects, against unreasonable searches and seizures, shall not be violated, and no Warrants shall issue, but upon probable cause, supported by Oath or affirmation, and particularly describing the place to be searched, and the persons or things to be seized.

Amendment V [1791]

No person shall be . . . compelled in any criminal case to be a witness against himself, nor be deprived of life, liberty, or property, without due process of law; nor shall private property be taken for public use, without just compensation.

Amendment VIII [1791]

Excessive bail shall not be required, nor excessive fines imposed, nor cruel and unusual punishments inflicted.

Amendment IX [1791]

The enumeration in the Constitution, of certain rights, shall not be construed to deny or disparage others retained by the people.

Amendment X [1791]

The powers not delegated to the United States by the Constitution, nor prohibited by it to the States, are reserved to the States respectively, or to the people.

Amendment XIV [1868]

Section 1. All persons born or naturalized in the United States, and subject to the jurisdiction thereof, are citizens of the United States and of the State wherein they reside. No State shall make or enforce any law which shall abridge the privileges or immunities of citizens of the United States; nor shall any State deprive any person of life, liberty, or property, without due process of law; nor deny to any person within its jurisdiction the equal protection of the laws.

Section 5. The Congress shall have power to enforce, by appropriate legislation, the provisions of this article.

Major Federal Laws Affecting Schools

Overview of Major Federal Statutes Related to Elementary and Secondary Schools

Statute	Principal Purpose
Individuals with Disabilities Education Act, 20 U.S.C. § 1400 *et seq.*	Ensures that students with disabilities will receive a free appropriate public education.
Section 504 of the Rehabilitation Act, 29 U.S.C. § 794	Prohibits discrimination based on disability in programs offered by recipients of any federal funds.
Title IX of the Education Amendments of 1972, 20 U.S.C. § 1681 *et seq.*	Prohibits discrimination based on gender in educational programs or activities offered by recipients of any federal funds.
Age Discrimination in Employment Act, 29 U.S.C. § 621 *et seq.*	Prohibits discrimination in employment against employees age 40 years and older.
Title VI of the Civil Rights Act of 1964, 42 U.S.C. § 2000d *et seq.*	Prohibits discrimination based on race, color, or national origin by recipients of any federal funds.
Title VII of the Civil Rights Act of 1964, 42 U.S.C. § 2000e *et seq.*	Prohibits discrimination based on race, color, national origin, religion, or sex by both private and public employers.
Family and Medical Leave Act of 1993, 29 U.S.C. § 2601 *et seq.*	Permits employees up to 12 weeks of unpaid leave for serious personal or family illnesses and for the birth or adoption of a child.
Americans with Disabilities Act, 42 U.S.C. § 12101 *et seq.*	Prohibits discrimination based on disability in employment, services, and accommodations by both private and public employers.
No Child Left Behind Act, 20 U.S.C. § 6301 *et seq.*	Creates a comprehensive system of ensuring accountability by local school systems for educational achievement by every student.

Statute	Principal Purpose
Family Educational Rights and Privacy Act, 20 U.S.C. § 1232g	Prohibits disclosure of students' educational records and provides access by students and parents to those records.
Paul D. Coverdell Teacher Protection Act of 2001, 20 U.S.C. § 6731	Limits civil liability for teachers and other school personnel who discipline students or maintain order or control in the school.
Civil Rights Act of 1871, 42 U.S.C. § 1983	Prohibits violation of federal laws or constitutional rights under color of state law.
Technology Education Copyright Harmonization Act of 2002, 17 U.S.C. § 110 *et seq.*	Expands available use of copyrighted materials for educational purposes, including electronically transmitted information.

Administrative agency. Any branch or division of the government other than the judicial or legislative branches (such as the Social Security Administration or the Department of Education).

Administrative law. Regulations and procedures that govern the operation of administrative agencies.

Adversary system. System of law in the United States whereby the truth is thought to be best revealed through a clash in the courtroom between opposite sides to a dispute.

Affidavit. A written statement sworn to before a person officially permitted by law to administer an oath.

Amicus curiae. "Friend of the court"; a person or organization allowed to appear in a lawsuit, to file arguments in the form of a brief supporting one side or the other, even though not party to the dispute.

Answer. The first pleading by the defendant in a lawsuit. This statement sets forth the defendant's responses to the charges contained in the plaintiffs "complaint."

Appeal. Asking a higher court to review the actions of a lower court in order to correct mistakes or injustice.

Appellate court. A court having jurisdiction to review the actions of an inferior court (such as a trial court) but not having the power to hear a legal action initially.

Appellee. See *Defendant.*

Beyond a reasonable doubt. The level of proof required to convict a person of a crime. This is the highest level of proof required in any type of trial, in contrast to *by a fair preponderance of the evidence,* the level of proof in civil cases.

Bill of Rights. The first ten amendments to the U.S. Constitution.

Brief. A written summary or condensed statement of a case. Also a written statement prepared by one side in a lawsuit to explain its case to the judge.

By a fair preponderance of the evidence. The level of proof required in a civil case. This level is lower than that required in criminal cases.

Cause of action. Facts sufficient to allow a valid lawsuit to proceed.

Certiorari. A request for review of a lower court decision, which the higher court can refuse.

Circumstantial evidence. Evidence that indirectly proves a main fact in question. Such evidence is open to doubt, since it is inferential—for example, a student seen in the vicinity of the locker room at the time of a theft is the thief.

Civil case. Every lawsuit other than a criminal proceeding. Most civil cases involve a lawsuit brought by one person against another and usually concern money damages.

Class action. A lawsuit brought by one person on behalf of himself or herself and all other persons in the same situation; persons bringing such suits must meet certain statutory criteria and must follow certain notice procedures.

Code. A collection of laws. Most states have an education code containing all laws directly relevant to education.

Common law. Law made by judges (as opposed to law made by legislatures).

Compensatory damages. Damages that relate to the actual loss suffered by a plaintiff, such as loss of income.

Complaint. The first main paper filed in a civil lawsuit. It includes, among other things, a statement of the wrong or harm done to the plaintiff by the defendant and a request for specific help from the court. The defendant responds to the complaint by filing an "answer."

Concurring opinion. Agrees with the majority opinion but gives different or added reasons for arriving at that opinion.

Criminal case. Cases involving crimes against the laws of the state; unlike in civil cases, the state is the prosecuting party.

De facto. In fact, actual; a situation that exists in fact whether or not it is lawful. *De facto* segregation is that which exists regardless of the law or the actions of civil authorities.

Defamation. Injuring a person's character or reputation by false or malicious statements. This includes both *libel* and *slander.*

Defendant (appellee). The person against whom a legal action is brought. This legal action may be civil or criminal. At the appeal stage, the party against whom an appeal is taken is known as the *appellee.*

De jure. Of right, legitimate; lawful. *De jure* segregation is that which is sanctioned by law.

De minimus. Small, unimportant; not worthy of concern.

Demurrer. The formal means by which one party to a lawsuit argues against the legal sufficiency of the other party's claim. A demurrer basically contends that even if all the facts that the other party alleges are true, they do not constitute a legal cause of action.

De novo. Completely new from the start; for example: a trial *de novo* is a completely new trial ordered by the trial judge or by an appeals court.

Dictum. A digression; a discussion of side points or unrelated points. Short for *obiter dictum;* plural is *dicta.*

Disclaimer. The refusal to accept certain types of responsibility. For example, a college catalog may disclaim any responsibility for guaranteeing that the courses contained therein will actually be offered, since courses, programs, and instructors are likely to change without notice.

Dissenting opinion. Disagrees with the majority opinion.

En banc. In the bench. The full panel of judges assigned to a court sit to hear a case, usually a case of special significance.

Equity. Fairness; the name of a type of court originating in England to handle legal problems when the existing laws did not cover some situations in which a person's rights were violated by another person. In the United States, civil courts have the powers of both law and equity. If only money is represented in a case, the court is acting as a law court and will give only monetary relief. If something other than money is requested—injunction, declaratory judgment, specific performance of a contractual agreement, etc.—then the court takes jurisdiction in equity and will grant a decree ordering acts to be done or not done. There is no jury in an equity case. Actions at law and suits in equity involve civil cases, not criminal.

Et al. "And others." When the words *et al.* are used in an opinion, the court is thereby indicating that there are unnamed parties, either plaintiffs or defendants, also before the court in the case.

Ex parte. With only one side present; an *ex parte* judicial proceeding involves only one party without notice to, or contestation by, any person adversely affected.

Ex post facto law. A law that retroactively changes the legal consequences of an act that has already been performed. Article 1, section 10 of the U.S. Constitution forbids the passage of *ex post facto* laws.

. . . .

157

Expunge.   Blot out. For example, a court order requesting that a student's record be expunged of any references to disciplinary action means that the references are to be "wiped off the books."

Ex rel.   On behalf of, when a case is titled *State ex rel. Doe v. Roe,* it means that the state is bringing a lawsuit against Roe on behalf of Doe.

Fiduciary.   A relationship between persons in which one person acts for another in a position of trust.

Guardian ad litem.   A guardian appointed by a court to represent a minor unable to represent him or herself.

Hearing.   An oral proceeding before a court or quasi-judicial tribunal. Hearings that describe a process to ascertain facts and provide evidence are labeled "trial-like hearings" or simply "trials." Hearings that relate to a presentation of ideas as distinguished from facts and evidence are known as "arguments." The former occur in trial courts and the latter occur in appellate courts. The terms "trial," "trial-like hearing," "quasi-judicial hearing," "evidentiary hearing," and "adjudicatory hearing" are all used by courts and have overlapping meanings. See *Trial.*

Hearsay.   Secondhand evidence; facts not in the personal knowledge of the witness but a repetition of what others said that is used to prove the truth of what those others said. Hearsay is generally not allowed as evidence at a trial, although there are many exceptions.

Holding.   The rule of law in a case; that part of the judge's written opinion that applies the law to the facts of the case and about which can be said "the case means no more and no less than this." A holding is the opposite of *dictum.*

In camera.   "In chambers"; in a judge's private office; a hearing in court with all spectators excluded.

Incriminate.   To involve in a crime, to cause to appear guilty.

Informed consent.   A person's agreement to allow something to happen (such as being the subject of a research study) that is based on a full disclosure of facts needed to make the decision intelligently.

Injunction.   A court order requiring someone to do something or refrain from taking some action.

In loco parentis.   In place of the parent; acting as a parent with respect to the care, supervision, and discipline of a child.

In re.   In the matter of. This is a prefix to the name of a case, often used when a child is involved. For example, "*In re John Jones*" might be the title of a child neglect proceeding though it is really against the parents.

Ipso facto.   By the fact itself, by the mere fact that.

Judicial review.   The power of a court to declare a statute unconstitutional; also the power to interpret the meaning of laws.

Jurisdiction.   A court's authority to hear a case; also the geographical area within which a court has the right and power to operate. Original jurisdiction means that the court will be the first to hear the case; appellate jurisdiction means that the court reviews cases on appeal from lower court rulings.

Law.   Basic rules of order as pronounced by a government. Common law refers to laws originating in custom or practice. Statute law refers to laws passed by legislatures and recorded in public documents. Case law are the pronouncements of courts.

Libel. Written defamation; published false and malicious written statements that injure a person's reputation.

Mandamus. A writ issued by a court commanding that some official duty be performed.

Material. Important, going to the heart of the matter; for example, a material fact is one necessary to reach a decision.

Misrepresentation. A false statement; if knowingly made, misrepresentation may be illegal and result in punishment.

Mitigation. The reduction in a fine, penalty, sentence, or damages initially assessed or decreed against a defendant.

Moot. Abstract; not a real case involving a real dispute.

Motion. A request made by a lawyer that a judge take certain action, such as dismissing a case.

Majority opinion. The opinion agreed on by more than half the judges or justices hearing a case, sometimes called the opinion of the court.

Ordinance. The term applied to a municipal corporation's legislative enactments.

Parens patriae. Parent of the country; the historical right of all governments to take care of persons under their jurisdiction, particularly minors and incapacitated persons.

Per curiam. An unsigned decision and opinion of a court, as distinguished from one signed by a judge.

Petitioner. One who initiates a proceeding and requests that some relief be granted on his or her behalf. A plaintiff. When the term *petitioner* is used, the one against whom the petitioner is complaining is referred to as the *respondent.*

Plaintiff. One who initiates a lawsuit; the party bringing suit.

Pleading. The process of making formal, written statements of each side of a case. First the plaintiff submits a paper with facts and claims; then the defendant submits a paper with facts and counterclaims; then the plaintiff responds; and so on until all issues and questions are clearly posed for a trial.

Political question. A question that the courts will not decide because it concerns a decision more properly made by another branch of government, such as the legislature.

Precedent. A court decision on a question of law that gives authority or direction on how to decide a similar question of law in a later case with similar facts.

Prima facie. Clear on the face of it; presumably, a fact that will be considered to be true unless disproved by contrary evidence. For example, a *prima facie* case is a case that will win unless the other side comes forward with evidence to dispute it.

Punitive damages. Money awarded to a person by a court that is over and above the damages actually sustained. Punitive damages are designed to serve as a deterrent to similar acts in the future.

Quasi-judicial. The case-deciding function of an administrative agency.

Redress. To set right, remedy, make up for, remove the cause of a complaint or grievance.

Remand. Send back. A higher court may remand a case to a lower court with instructions to take some action in the case.

Res judicata. A thing decided. Thus if a court decides a case, the matter is settled and no new lawsuit on the same subject may be brought by the persons involved.

Respondent. One who makes an answer in a legal appellate proceeding. This term is frequently used in appellate and divorce cases rather than the more customary term, *defendant.*

Sectarian. Characteristic of a sect or religion.

Secular. Not religious, ecclesiastical, or clerical; relating to the worldly or temporal.

Sine qua non. A thing or condition that is indispensable.

Slander. Oral defamation; the speaking of false and malicious words that injure another person's reputation, business, or property rights.

Sovereign immunity. The government's freedom from being sued for money damages without its consent.

Standing. A person's right to bring a lawsuit because he or she is directly affected by the issues raised.

Stare decisis. "Let the decision stand"; a legal rule that when a court has decided a case by applying a legal principle to a set of facts, that court should stick by that principle and apply it to all later cases with clearly similar facts unless there is a good reason not to. This rule helps promote predictability and reliability in judicial decision making and is inherent in the American legal system.

Statute of limitation. A statute that sets forth the time period within which litigation may be commenced in a particular cause of action.

Strict scrutiny. A stringent standard applied by the courts when a person's important constitutional right is restricted or denied by official action.

Tort. A civil wrong done by one person to another. For an act to be a tort, there must be a legal duty owed by one person to another, a breach of that duty, and harm done as a direct result of the action.

Trial. A process occurring in a court whereby opposing parties present evidence, which is subject to cross-examination and rebuttal, pertaining to the matter in dispute.

Trial court. The court in which a case is originally tried, as distinct from higher courts to which the case might be appealed.

Ultra vires. Going beyond the specifically delegated authority to act; for example, a school board which is by law restricted from punishing students for behavior occurring wholly off campus might act *ultra vires* in punishing a student for behavior observed at a private weekend party.

Waiver. An intentional or uncoerced release of a known right.

i n d e x